THE ULTIMATE GUIDE OF FUN THINGS TO DO IN RETIREMENT

ENJOYABLE AND STIMULATING ACTIVITIES TO MAKE NEW FRIENDS, IMPROVE MENTAL CLARITY, FIND NEW PASSIONS AND DIVE INTO GLOBAL ADVENTURES

VICTORIA BLAINE

VICTORIA BLAINE PUBLISHING

Copyright © 2024 by Victoria Blaine Publishing.
All rights reserved.
No part of this book may be reproduced in any form or by any electronic or mechanical means, including information storage and retrieval systems, without written permission from the author, except for the use of brief quotations in a book review.

CONTENTS

Introduction — vii

1. REDISCOVERING YOURSELF — 1
   Uncovering Hidden Passions — 2
   Creating Your Retirement Vision Board — 5
   Journaling for Self-Discovery — 9
   Embracing a Growth Mindset — 14
   Setting Personal Goals and Milestones — 17

2. SOCIAL CONNECTIONS AND FRIENDSHIPS — 21
   Hosting Themed Social Gatherings — 25
   Using Technology to Stay Connected — 28
   Starting or Joining a Book Club — 32
   Volunteering for Social Good — 35

3. TRAVEL AND ADVENTURE — 40
   Traveling on the Open Road — 41
   Exploring International Volunteer Vacations — 45
   Group Travel: Tours and Cruises — 49
   Adventure Travel for the Thrill-Seeker — 52
   Cultural Immersion Trips — 56

4. CREATIVE AND ARTISTIC PURSUITS	61
Painting and Drawing for Beginners	62
Writing Your Memoirs or a Novel	65
Crafting with Recycled Materials	69
Photography: Capturing Life's Moments	72
Music and Dance: Learning an Instrument or Dance Style	76
5. HEALTH AND FITNESS	81
Low-Impact Exercises for Joint Health	82
Yoga and Meditation for Mind-Body Balance	87
Swimming and Water Aerobics	90
Joining a Walking or Hiking Group	94
Pickleball for Seniors	97
Nutrition Tips for Active Seniors	101
6. LIFELONG LEARNING AND EDUCATION	108
Enrolling in Online Courses	109
Attending Local Workshops and Seminars	113
Learning a New Language	117
Exploring History Through Local Museums	121
Joining a Community College Class	125

7. VOLUNTEERING AND
   GIVING BACK   130
   Finding the Right Volunteer
   Opportunity   131
   Mentoring and Tutoring Programs   135
   Environmental Conservation
   Projects   138
   Participating in Local Charity Events   142
   Voluntourism: Combining Travel
   and Volunteering   146

8. FINANCIAL PEACE OF MIND   151
   Budgeting for Your New Lifestyle   152
   Exploring Part-Time Work and
   Freelance Opportunities   155
   Maximizing Social Security Benefits   159
   Downsizing and Simplifying
   Your Home   164
   Smart Investing for Retirees   167

9. TECHNOLOGY AND DIGITAL
   SKILLS   172
   Mastering Social Media Platforms   173
   Creating and Maintaining a Blog   176
   Using Apps for Health and Fitness
   Tracking   180
   Online Safety and Privacy Tips   185
   Virtual Socializing: Zoom and
   Beyond   188

10. MENTAL WELL-BEING AND
    MINDFULNESS   193
    Meditation Techniques for
    Beginners   194
    Engaging in Brain Games and
    Puzzles   200
    Practicing Gratitude and Positive
    Thinking   205

    Conclusion   213
    References   219

INTRODUCTION

Let's start with a story. Meet Linda, a recent retiree who was once a dedicated schoolteacher. After decades of shaping young minds, she found herself sitting at home, staring at the walls and wondering what to do next. She felt a mix of excitement and dread. Would she find joy in this new chapter or be stuck in a rut of endless TV marathons? Linda's journey is one many retirees face. It's a time filled with potential but also with uncertainty.

This book aims to take that uncertainty and turn it into excitement. We'll explore countless ideas and activities that can make your retirement fulfilling and downright joyful. Whether you're into gardening, volunteering, or learning a new language, there's something here for everyone. This book aims to be your go-to guide for a fun and engaging retirement.

My vision for this book is simple: I want you to see retirement as the best time of your life. Think outside the box. Try something new. Discover talents you never knew you had. Retirement is your time to shine, to reinvent yourself, and to enjoy every moment.

In this book, I will share a number of ideas on how to spend this amazing time in your life. Think about these ideas. Do they sound like something that might interest you? If so, read further and delve into the suggestions on how to learn more. Read through the real-life examples. These personal stories are designed to inspire and share how others have found joy and fulfillment during this fantastic time. Keep an open mind and truly open yourself up to exploring new and exciting opportunities.

Of course, retirement isn't without its challenges. Many retirees worry about boredom, loneliness, and a lack of purpose. You may be asking yourself, "What now?" or "How do I fill my days?" This book will address these concerns head-on. We'll look at ways to keep your mind sharp, your social calendar full, and your sense of purpose strong.

So, what's in it for you? To begin, enhanced social connections. We'll explore activities that get you out and about, meeting new people and strengthening old friendships. Improved mental health is another biggie. Engaging in meaningful activities can boost your mood and keep your mind agile. And let's not forget a renewed sense of purpose. Finding something you're passionate about can give you a reason to get out of bed each morning.

We'll cover a range of themes and topics. Travel is a big one—whether you're exploring new countries or rediscovering your own backyard. Hobbies like painting, gardening, or even drone flying can add spice to your days. Volunteering offers a way to give back while feeling good about yourself. Lifelong learning keeps your brain engaged and curious. The possibilities are endless.

But it's not just about ideas; it's about action. This book promises practical, actionable advice. You'll find detailed examples and step-by-step guides to help you implement these ideas. We'll ensure you have all the tools to turn inspiration into reality.

I encourage you to engage with the content, try

new activities, take risks, and embrace the journey of self-discovery that retirement offers. This is your time to explore, grow, and enjoy.

Here's what you can expect in the upcoming chapters. We'll start with easy-to-try activities that require minimal effort but offer maximum joy. Then, we'll dive into more adventurous pursuits, from travel to new hobbies. The purpose of each chapter is to provide valuable guidance and inspiration, ensuring you find something that resonates with you.

Retirement is not the end; it's a new beginning. An opportunity for growth, adventure, and fulfillment. It's a chance to live life on your terms and pursue your passions. So, get ready. The best is yet to come!

Welcome to your new life. Let's make it extraordinary!

1

REDISCOVERING YOURSELF

"Retirement is not the end of work; it is the beginning of a new phase where you can focus on the things that truly matter."

— ALBERT EINSTEIN

When John retired as an engineer, he felt a sudden void—before, his days comprised meetings, project deadlines, and problem-solving challenges. Now, he had all the time in the world but no clear direction on how to use it. While cleaning his attic one afternoon, he stumbled upon an old box of watercolor paints and brushes. Memories of his younger self, spending hours painting landscapes and still life, flooded back. Inspired, John decided to take up painting again. What started as a simple pastime soon became a passion that filled his days with joy and creativity. John's story is a testament to the power of rediscovering old hobbies and interests.

This chapter is all about finding those hidden passions you might have set aside during the hustle and bustle of your working years. Whether it's a childhood hobby, a long-forgotten ambition, or an activity you enjoyed on vacation, now is the perfect time to revisit these interests. It involves looking back to move forward, finding joy in activities that once brought you happiness, and even discovering new ones.

Uncovering Hidden Passions

Think back to your childhood. What did you enjoy doing before life got in the way? Maybe you loved painting, playing an instrument, or building model airplanes. These hobbies often take a backseat as we grow older and responsibilities pile up. But now, with more free time, you can reignite those passions. Learning a new language or writing a book can find their place in your life again. And remember those activities you enjoyed during vacations, like snorkeling, hiking, or birdwatching. Each of these interests has the potential to become a fulfilling part of your retirement.

To help uncover these hidden passions, start by asking yourself a few questions. What activities did you enjoy as a child or teenager? Think about the hobbies you've always wanted to try but have not had time for. What topics or activities make you lose track of time? Reflecting on these questions can provide valuable insights. Maybe you used to love gardening but stopped because of a busy schedule. Or you've always been fascinated by photography but never picked up a camera. These reflections can be the first step toward rediscovering yourself.

Practical exercises can also help explore new interests. Consider sampling different hobbies through community classes. Local community centers often offer a variety of courses, from pottery and painting to dance and music. Attending local events or workshops can expose you to new activities and like-minded individuals. Don't hesitate to experiment with do-it-yourself (DIY) projects at home. Whether building a birdhouse, knitting a scarf, or trying out new recipes, these activities can be fun and rewarding.

Let's look at some real-life examples for inspiration. Take the story of Barbara, a retiree who discovered a love for photography. She started with a basic camera and took a few classes at a local community college. Gradually, her interest grew, and she began exploring different photography genres, from landscapes to portraits. Today, Barbara's photographs are displayed in local galleries, and she has won a few awards. Her journey began with simple curiosity and evolved into a passionate pursuit.

Another example is Tom, who took up gardening for the first time after retirement. Tom had always admired beautiful gardens but didn't have enough time or space to create one. After moving to a house with a backyard, he decided to try it. He started small, planting a few flowers and vegetables. The joy of watching his garden grow, coupled with the physical activity and fresh air, transformed his daily routine. Gardening became a source of relaxation and pride for Tom, proving that it's always possible to start something new.

Rediscovering hidden passions is about giving yourself permission to explore and enjoy. It means looking back at what made you happy and finding ways to incorporate those activities into your life. The possibilities are endless, whether it's picking up a paintbrush, learning to play the piano, or trying your hand at woodworking. Retirement is your time to explore, try new things, and find joy in activities that make your heart sing. So, take the first step and rediscover the passions that await you.

Creating Your Retirement Vision Board

Picture yourself in a room surrounded by images of tropical beaches, cozy reading nooks, vibrant gardens, and joyful family gatherings. Each of these pictures symbolizes a dream, goal, or aspiration. This is the core of a vision board—a powerful tool to help you visualize and realize your retirement dreams. A vision board is a daily reminder of your goals and is a source of motivation and focus. It offers a tangible representation of your dreams, making them feel more attainable and definite.

. . .

Creating a vision board is a straightforward process, but its impact can be profound. Start by gathering magazines, newspapers, and any printed materials that catch your eye. Flip through these pages and cut out images, words, and quotes that resonate with you. Look for pictures that evoke a sense of joy, excitement, or peace. These could be images of places you want to visit, activities you want to try, or even the lifestyle you envision for yourself. If you prefer a digital approach, platforms like Pinterest offer a convenient way to collect and organize your vision. Create boards for different themes and pin images from the internet that align with your goals.

Once you have a collection of images and quotes, it's time to assemble your vision board. Find a large poster board or corkboard and start arranging your cutouts. Group similar items together to create a cohesive and visually appealing layout. Place all your travel aspirations in one section, health and fitness goals in another, and creative projects in another. Use personal photos to add a touch of individuality to your board. Seeing yourself in these images can make your dreams feel even more attainable.

Maintaining and updating your vision board is crucial to keeping it relevant and inspiring. Regularly add new images and quotes as your goals evolve. You may come across a stunning picture of a place you've never considered visiting or find a quote that perfectly encapsulates your current mindset. Incorporate these new elements into your board to keep it fresh and motivating. Periodically review and reflect on your vision board. This reflection can help you focus on your goals and remind you of your progress.

Categorizing your vision board into different life areas can make it more organized and effective. If you have travel aspirations, let's start there. Pin images of places you'd like to visit, be it a lively city, a tranquil beach, or a scenic mountain range. Next, think about your health and fitness goals. Include images that inspire you to stay active and healthy, like people doing yoga, nutritious meals, or nature trails perfect for hiking. Creative projects and hobbies are another vital area. Whether it's painting, knitting, or writing, find images representing these activities and place them prominently on your board.

~

Interactive Element: Creating Your Vision Board

1. **Gather Materials:** Magazines, newspapers, scissors, glue, poster board, or corkboard.
2. **Select Images:** Cut out pictures, words, and quotes that resonate with your goals.
3. **Organize:** Group similar items together, such as travel, health, and hobbies.
4. **Assemble:** Glue or pin your selections onto the board, creating a visually appealing layout.
5. **Personalize:** Add personal photos to make your vision board uniquely yours.
6. **Update Regularly:** Add new images and quotes as your goals evolve.
7. **Reflect Periodically:** Review your board to stay focused and motivated.

Note: If you are more computer savvy, you can create a vision board digitally. The choice is yours!

A vision board is more than just a collage of pretty pictures; it's a tool that helps you focus on what truly matters to you. It's a daily reminder of the life you want to lead and the goals you aim to achieve. Visualizing your dreams makes you more likely to take the steps needed to make them a reality. Creating and maintaining a vision board can be inspiring and empowering, whether you choose a physical or digital board. So, gather your materials, let your imagination run wild, and start crafting your vision for a fulfilling and joyful retirement.

Journaling for Self-Discovery

Envision yourself with a cup of tea, a blank notebook, and a pen. As you start writing about your day, thoughts, and dreams, you engage in the simple yet powerful act of journaling. This process allows you to explore your thoughts and emotions, enhancing your self-awareness. Journaling allows you to reflect on your experiences, identify patterns, and understand what truly brings you joy. It's a method for connecting with yourself on a deeper level, reducing stress and anxiety. Your goals and aspirations may become more apparent as you write, making it easier to shape a fulfilling retirement.

To get started with journaling, consider using prompts to guide your writing. These prompts can spark your creativity and help you explore different aspects of your life. For example, ask yourself, "What does a perfect day in retirement look like for me?"

Visualize your ideal day from morning to night and describe it in detail. Another prompt could be, "List three activities that make you feel truly alive." Reflect on the moments when you felt most engaged and energized. Finally, try, "Reflect on a recent experience that brought you joy." Describe the event, how it made you feel, and why it was meaningful to you. These prompts can help you uncover insights about yourself and your desires.

There are various journaling techniques and formats to explore, each offering benefits. Freewriting involves writing continuously without worrying about grammar or punctuation. It allows your thoughts to flow freely, often leading to surprising discoveries. Bullet journaling combines traditional journaling and task management, using bullet points to organize your thoughts and goals. This method can help you stay focused and productive. Gratitude journaling is another popular technique where you write down things you're grateful for daily. This practice can shift your mindset to a more positive outlook, enhancing overall well-being.

Consider the story of Margaret, a retiree who found clarity through journaling. She began by writing about her daily experiences, gradually uncovering her values and passions. Over time, Margaret realized she had always wanted to volunteer at a local animal shelter. Journaling helped her articulate this desire, and she eventually took the plunge, finding immense satisfaction in her new role.

Another example is Robert, who used journaling to set and achieve new goals. He started with a simple list of aspirations, such as learning to play the guitar and traveling to Italy. By documenting his progress and reflecting on his experiences,

Robert stayed motivated and achieved his goals, enriching his retirement years.

Journaling is a flexible and personal practice, allowing you to find a style that suits your needs. Consistency is critical, whether you prefer freewriting, bullet journaling, or gratitude journaling. Set aside a few minutes each day to write, making it a regular part of your routine. You don't need to write lengthy entries; even a few sentences can be impactful. Writing matters—it helps you process your thoughts and emotions, leading to greater self-awareness and clarity.

If you're new to journaling, start with simple prompts and exercises. Write about your dreams, goals, fears, challenges, joys, and successes. Use your journal as a safe space to explore your inner world, free from judgment. Over time, you may find that journaling becomes a cherished habit, offering you insights and guidance as you navigate this new chapter of your life.

∼

To keep your journaling practice engaging:

1. Vary your prompts and techniques.
2. Experiment with different formats, such as list-making, mind mapping, or even incorporating drawings and sketches.
3. Reflect on your entries periodically, noticing any patterns or themes that emerge.
4. Share your experiences with others if you feel comfortable. Discussing your reflections can deepen your understanding and provide new perspectives.

～

Journaling can be a transformative tool for self-discovery in retirement. It helps you connect with yourself, clarify your goals, and navigate the complexities of this new phase of life. Whether you're reflecting on your perfect day, listing activities that bring you joy, or exploring different journaling techniques, the process can lead to meaningful insights and personal growth. So, grab a notebook and pen and start your journaling journey today.

Embracing a Growth Mindset

Picture yourself in a garden, cultivating plants that grow and flourish with the proper care and attention. This visualization is much like adopting a growth mindset in retirement. A growth mindset is the belief that developing abilities and intelligence through dedication and hard work is possible. This concept, introduced by psychologist Carol Dweck, is particularly significant in retirement. It fosters continuous personal growth, resilience, and adaptability. Embracing a growth mindset can transform how you approach this new phase of life, opening doors to endless possibilities and enriching your retirement experience.

Learning and development are at the core of a growth mindset. Retirement offers the perfect opportunity to explore new areas of interest and deepen your knowledge. Whether picking up a new hobby, mastering a skill, or even pursuing further education, the value lies in learning. This mindset keeps your brain active and brings a sense of accomplishment and purpose. It encourages you to view challenges as opportunities for growth rather than obstacles, promoting a positive and proactive approach to life.

. . .

To cultivate a growth mindset, start by challenging self-limiting beliefs. These thoughts tell you, "I can't do this" or "I'm too old to learn." Replace them with empowering affirmations like, "I can improve with practice" or "It's never too late to learn something new." Setting incremental goals can also help. Break down larger objectives into smaller, manageable steps, and celebrate your progress. This step keeps you motivated and also builds confidence in your abilities. Seeking feedback and learning from experiences is another important strategy. Constructive criticism offers valuable insights and helps refine your approach, leading to better outcomes.

Lifelong learning plays a vital role in fostering a growth mindset. Enroll in online courses that pique your interest. Platforms like Coursera, Udemy, and edX offer various subjects, from art and history to technology and science. These courses can be taken at your own pace, making them flexible and convenient. Attending workshops and seminars is another excellent way to stay engaged and curious. Local community centers, libraries, and universities often host events on various topics. Reading and exploring new subjects can also keep your mind sharp. Dive into books, articles, and documentaries that expand your horizons and stimulate your intellect.

Consider the story of Mary, a retiree who decided to learn digital photography. Initially, Mary felt overwhelmed by the technical aspects of using a camera and editing software. However, she approached it with a growth mindset, taking online courses and seeking feedback from fellow photographers. Her skills improved slowly, and Mary began capturing stunning images. Today, Mary's photographs are featured in local art shows, and she has even started teaching photography classes. Her story illustrates how a growth mindset can lead to mastering new skills and finding new passions.

Another inspiring example is James, who faced significant health challenges after retirement. Instead of letting these obstacles deter him, James adopted a growth mindset. He set small, achievable goals for his recovery and celebrated each milestone, no matter how small. James also sought feedback from his physical therapists and learned from his setbacks. Over time, his resilience and adaptability paid off, and he regained much of his strength and mobility. James's journey demonstrates how a growth mindset can help overcome challenges and lead to personal triumphs.

Embracing a growth mindset in retirement means staying curious, open-minded, and willing to learn. It's seeing every experience as an opportunity for growth and viewing challenges as stepping stones to success. This mindset enhances your abilities and enriches your life, making retirement a time of continuous discovery and fulfillment.

Setting Personal Goals and Milestones

Setting clear, attainable goals in retirement can be a game-changer. It provides direction and purpose, transforming what might seem like endless free time into a series of meaningful, fulfilling pursuits. Imagine waking up each day with a plan, knowing that you're working toward something significant. Goals create a sense of achievement and keep you motivated and engaged. They turn abstract dreams into concrete steps, giving you a roadmap to follow.

. . .

To make your goals effective, consider the SMART framework: Specific, Measurable, Achievable, Relevant, and Time-bound. This approach ensures your goals are clear and reachable. For example, instead of saying, "I want to get fit," a SMART goal would be, "I will walk thirty minutes every morning for the next three months." This goal is specific (walking thirty minutes), measurable (thirty minutes), achievable (a reasonable amount of time), relevant (improves fitness), and time-bound (three months). Breaking down large goals into manageable steps can make them less daunting and more achievable. Start with short-term goals that lead to long-term achievements. Regularly review and adjust these goals to align with your evolving interests and capabilities.

Milestones play a crucial role in tracking progress. They act as markers that keep you on track and motivated. Creating a timeline for achieving your goals helps visualize the journey and maintain momentum. Use milestone markers to celebrate small victories along the way. For instance, if you want to write a book, celebrate the completion of each chapter. These small rewards reinforce your progress and keep you motivated. Rewarding yourself for reaching milestones can be as simple as taking a day off to relax or treating yourself to something special. It means recognizing your efforts and celebrating the progress you've made.

Consider the story of David, a retiree who set and achieved fitness goals. David decided he wanted to run a 5K race. He started with a SMART goal: "I will jog three times a week for twenty minutes each session for the next six weeks." He broke this down into smaller steps, gradually increasing his jogging time. David created a timeline and marked each week's progress. When he reached his first milestone of jogging for twenty minutes without stopping, he rewarded himself with a new pair of running shoes. By the end of six weeks, David had completed a 5K and discovered a newfound love for running. His journey highlights the power of setting clear goals and celebrating milestones.

Another inspiring example is Susan, who pursued a creative project step by step. Susan has always wanted to learn to paint but never had the time. She set a goal in retirement: "I will complete one painting each month for the next year." She started by taking a beginner's painting class, setting short-term goals like learning basic techniques and completing her first canvas. Each completed painting was a milestone, and she celebrated by displaying her work in her home gallery. By the end of the year, Susan had twelve beautiful paintings and had developed a deep passion for art. Her story demonstrates how setting and achieving goals can lead to personal fulfillment and joy.

Setting personal goals and milestones in retirement isn't just about ticking boxes; it's about creating a life filled with purpose and satisfaction. It's about waking up each day with a sense of direction and knowing that every step you take leads you closer to your dreams. Whether it's achieving fitness goals like David's or pursuing creative projects like Susan's, the process of setting and working toward goals can transform your retirement into a time of growth and accomplishment. Embrace this opportunity to set your goals, track your progress, and celebrate your achievements. The possibilities are limitless, and the rewards are immeasurable. Now that you have an idea of your potential interests and passions let's explore how you can add social connections and friendships to the mix.

2

SOCIAL CONNECTIONS AND FRIENDSHIPS

"When we feel love and kindness toward others, it not only makes others feel loved and cared for, but it helps us also to develop inner happiness and peace."

— DALAI LAMA

Imagine this: You walk into a bustling community center, and the room is filled with laughter and animated conversation. People are playing cards, working on crafts, and sharing stories. You feel a sense of excitement and curiosity. This could be where new friendships blossom and old interests are rekindled. Social connections are vital, especially in retirement. They provide a sense of belonging and can make this phase of life more enjoyable and fulfilling.

Joining local clubs and organizations offers numerous benefits. It's an excellent way to meet like-minded individuals who share your interests. Whether you're passionate about gardening, knitting, or hiking, there's probably a club for you. These groups often organize regular social activities and events, giving you something to look forward to each week. Being part of a supportive network can also enhance your overall well-being. You'll have people who can provide encouragement, celebrate your achievements, and share your experiences. It's like having an extended family that shares your hobbies and passions.

Finding and joining local clubs is easier than you might think. Start by visiting your community center or checking local library and café bulletin boards. These places often have flyers and brochures about various clubs and organizations in your area. Online platforms like Meetup.com are another great resource. Meetup allows you to search for groups based on your interests and location. You can find everything from hiking clubs to book discussion groups. Local newspapers and magazines also list upcoming events and club meetings. Feel free to contact organizers or attend a meeting to see if the group is a good fit for you.

There's a wide variety of clubs and organizations to consider. Hobby clubs cater to specific interests like gardening, knitting, or photography. These clubs often have workshops, guest speakers, and hands-on activities that deepen your knowledge and skills. Sports teams and fitness groups provide an opportunity to stay active and healthy while enjoying the camaraderie of team sports or group exercises. Cultural and arts organizations offer a chance to explore new perspectives through theater, music, dance, and visual arts. These groups often organize outings to performances, exhibitions, and cultural events, enriching your retirement experience.

Take the story of Jane, who found lifelong friends through a hiking club. Jane had always enjoyed the outdoors but rarely had the time to hike during her working years. After retiring, she joined a local hiking group she found on Meetup. The group met every Saturday and explored different trails around the region. Jane improved her physical fitness and made close friends who shared her love of nature. They now plan hiking trips together and even volunteer for local conservation projects. Jane's weekends are filled with adventure and laughter, thanks to the connections she made through the club.

Similarly, consider Tom, who discovered a new passion through a local theater group. Tom had never acted before but decided to give it a try after seeing a notice at his community center. The group welcomed him with open arms and offered plenty of support as he learned the ropes. Tom quickly fell in love with acting and the thrill of performing on stage. He made friends who shared his enthusiasm and encouraged him to take on more challenging roles. Today, Tom is a regular in community theater productions, finding joy and fulfillment in something he never imagined he'd enjoy.

Joining local clubs and organizations can transform your retirement. It opens doors to new experiences, friendships, and opportunities for personal growth. Whether you're rekindling an old passion or discovering something new, these groups provide a sense of community and belonging. So, take the first step. Explore what's available in your area and find a club or organization that sparks your interest. The connections you make, and the experiences you share will enrich your life in ways you never thought possible.

Hosting Themed Social Gatherings

Visualize your living room as a lively hub of activity, filled with laughter, conversation, and the cheerful clinking of glasses. Themed social gatherings can create these unforgettable moments, fostering deeper connections among both old friends and new acquaintances. Adding a theme brings a fun and engaging vibe that encourages participation and interaction. A themed event naturally facilitates socializing, ensuring everyone feels included and engaged.

One popular idea is to host potluck dinners with an international cuisine theme. Invite your friends to bring dishes from different countries, turning the evening into a culinary adventure. This introduces everyone to new flavors and sparks exciting conversations about travel and culture. Another engaging option is a game night featuring classic and modern board games. Whether it's Scrabble, Monopoly, or the latest strategy game, these evenings can be filled with friendly competition and lots of laughs.

Crafting parties are perfect for DIY enthusiasts. Gather your friends for a fun afternoon of creating something beautiful. Whether making holiday decorations, painting pottery, or assembling scrapbooks, the shared crafting experience can be incredibly bonding. Movie nights featuring classic films or new releases offer a more relaxed option. Set up a cozy space with comfortable seating and popcorn, and let the magic of cinema bring everyone together.

Planning and hosting these gatherings doesn't have to be overwhelming. Start by creating and sending themed invitations. These can be simple yet creative, setting the tone for the event. For example, if you're hosting an international potluck, use images of world maps and flags in your invitation design. Setting up a comfortable and welcoming space is recommended. Arrange seating to encourage conversation and add decorations that enhance the theme. You might decorate with game pieces or themed tablecloths for a game night.

Activities and games are essential to keep guests entertained. Plan a few icebreakers to get everyone talking. During a potluck, you could have each guest share a fun fact about the country their dish represents. Consider having a tournament or team-based games that encourage collaboration for game nights. Movie nights can include trivia questions related to the film before the screening starts. The goal is to create an environment where everyone feels relaxed, engaged, and connected.

Consider the story of Helen, who regularly hosts book-themed dinners. Each month, she and her friends select a book to read and then gather for a dinner inspired by the book's setting or themes. For example, they read a novel set in Italy one month and enjoyed a delicious Italian feast together. These evenings are filled with rich discussions, laughter, and the joy of shared culinary and literary experiences. Helen's book-themed dinners have strengthened her friendships and provided a regular, anticipated event on everyone's calendar.

. . .

Another inspiring example is Mark, who organized a successful neighborhood block party. He wanted to bring his community closer, so he planned a summer barbecue with a carnival theme. Neighbors brought different dishes, and Mark set up simple games like a ring toss and a bean bag throw. The event was a hit, with people of all ages mingling and having a great time. Mark's block party created lasting memories and fostered a sense of community and support among his neighbors.

Hosting themed social gatherings can be an excellent way to strengthen social bonds and create lasting memories. These events provide a structured and engaging way to bring people together, fostering deeper connections and a sense of belonging. So, consider adding a theme to your next social gathering, whether it's a potluck dinner, game night, crafting party, or movie night. The effort you put into planning and hosting will be rewarded with laughter, connection, and joy.

Using Technology to Stay Connected

Think about the times you've wished you could see your loved ones more often or join in on their lives, even from a distance. Technology can bridge this gap, making it easier to maintain social connections no matter where you are. It facilitates communication with family and friends, enabling you to share moments, celebrate milestones, and offer support. This becomes particularly invaluable when physical distance separates you from those you care about. Moreover, technology opens doors to new communities and interests, helping you discover activities and groups that can enrich your social life.

Let's start with social media platforms, which have revolutionized how we stay connected. Setting up and using Facebook is straightforward, even for beginners. Begin by creating an account on Facebook's homepage. Fill in your basic details, such as your name, email, or phone number, and create a password. Once your account is set up, you can personalize your profile by adding a profile picture and cover photo. To connect with friends and family, use the search bar to find their profiles and send them friend requests. Once connected, you can share updates, photos, and videos on your timeline and interact with their posts by liking, commenting, or sharing.

. . .

Zoom has become a go-to tool for virtual gatherings and video calls. Download the Zoom app on your smartphone, tablet, or computer to get started. If you're using it for the first time, you'll need to sign up for a free account. Once installed, you can join a meeting by clicking on the link in the invitation email or entering the meeting ID on the app. Zoom's interface is user-friendly. You can join with or without video, and a mute button controls your microphone. The chat feature allows you to send messages during the meeting, making it easy to communicate even without speaking.

WhatsApp is another excellent tool for staying connected through instant messaging and group chats. Download the app from your app store and register using your phone number. Once set up, you can start individual chats or create group chats for family and friends. WhatsApp supports various forms of communication, including text messages, voice messages, video calls, and sharing photos and documents. It's a versatile platform that keeps you connected in real-time, no matter where you are.

. . .

Online communities and forums offer another layer of connection. These virtual spaces allow you to discuss topics of interest, share experiences, and seek advice from peers. They provide a platform where you can find support and encouragement and form bonds with people with similar interests or life experiences. Websites like Reddit, Gransnet, and various Facebook groups cater specifically to retirees, offering information and interaction opportunities. Engaging in these communities can be immensely rewarding, providing a sense of belonging and camaraderie.

Consider the story of Robert, a retiree who reconnected with old friends via social media. After joining Facebook, he searched for classmates from his high school days. He found several of them, to his delight, and started a group chat. They now regularly catch up, share memories, and even plan reunions. This reconnection has brought a new sense of joy and nostalgia to Robert's life, proving that it's always possible to revive old friendships.

. . .

Another inspiring example is Linda, who joined an online book club. She found the group through a social media platform and was initially hesitant about participating in virtual meetings. However, the experience turned out to be incredibly enriching. The book club members across different states meet weekly on Zoom to discuss their latest read. Linda has discovered new genres, made new friends, and looks forward to their lively discussions. The virtual format has kept her engaged and expanded her social circle beyond her local community.

Starting or Joining a Book Club

Think about settling into a cozy chair with a warm cup of tea and engaging in stimulating discussions about your latest read with like-minded individuals. A book club offers numerous benefits, fostering intellectual and social engagement. You explore diverse perspectives through lively conversations, enriching your understanding of various topics. This shared intellectual journey can spark new friendships as you bond over common interests and discover shared passions. Additionally, being part of a book club encourages regular reading habits, ensuring your mind is continuously nourished with fresh ideas and narratives.

. . .

Starting a book club can be an exciting endeavor and doesn't have to be complicated. Choose a theme or genre that interests you and your potential members. Whether it's mystery novels, historical fiction, or even nonfiction, having a focused theme helps attract people with similar tastes. Next, decide on a meeting schedule and location. Monthly meetings are a popular choice, giving everyone ample time to read the selected book. As for the location, consider rotating between members' homes or meeting at a local library or café. Setting guidelines for discussions and book selection is also important. Establish a respectful environment where everyone feels comfortable sharing their thoughts. Take turns suggesting books to ensure a diverse reading list.

If you're more interested in joining an existing book club, several resources can help you find the perfect fit. Community centers and libraries often host book clubs or can direct you to local groups. Online platforms like Goodreads have numerous book clubs catering to various genres and interests. You can join discussions, participate in polls, and even find virtual meetups. Don't hesitate to ask friends and family for recommendations; they may know of a club that would be a great match for you.

Consider the story of Alice, a retiree who found a sense of community through a local book club. Alice had always been an avid reader but missed having people to discuss her favorite books with. She discovered a book club at her local library and decided to join. The group met once a month and chose a different genre each time, keeping things fresh and exciting. Through the club, Alice met people who shared her love for literature and formed deep friendships over the years. The discussions were intellectually stimulating and provided a social outlet that enriched her retirement.

Another inspiring example is John, who joined a virtual book club that brought together readers from different countries. John had always been curious about how literature is perceived in various cultures. He found an online book club through Goodreads in which members from around the world discussed international literature. The virtual format allowed John to connect with people he would never have met otherwise, and the diverse perspectives broadened his understanding of global differences. The club's meetings on Zoom became a highlight of his month, offering both intellectual satisfaction and a sense of global camaraderie.

Book clubs can transform your reading experience into a social and intellectual adventure. They provide a platform to explore new ideas, challenge your thinking, and connect with others who share your passion for books. Whether you start your own club or join an existing one, the benefits are numerous. The friendships you form, the stimulating discussions you engage in, and the regular reading habits you develop will enrich your retirement in ways you never imagined. So, pick up that book you've been meaning to read and consider sharing your thoughts with fellow book lovers. The connections and insights you gain will make every page turn even more rewarding.

Volunteering for Social Good

Consider waking up each day with a sense of purpose, knowing that your actions are making a positive impact on the community. Volunteering provides this sense of fulfillment and much more, offering a unique opportunity to give back while enriching your life. Through volunteering, you can meet new people and build meaningful friendships. These connections create a supportive network, enhancing your sense of community and belonging. The fulfillment and satisfaction gained from helping others can significantly boost your mental and emotional well-being, making your retirement years even more rewarding.

Finding the right volunteer opportunity begins with assessing your skills and interests. Consider what you enjoy doing and where your strengths lie. Whether you're great with numbers, have a knack for organizing events, or possess a wealth of knowledge in a particular field, there's a volunteer position that can benefit from your expertise. Once you have a clear idea of your skills and interests, start researching local organizations and causes that resonate with you. Community centers, libraries, and local newspapers often list volunteer opportunities. Online platforms like VolunteerMatch can also help you find positions based on your preferences.

. . .

Reaching out to volunteer coordinators is an essential step in the process. These individuals can provide you with more detailed information about the roles available and what they entail. Feel free to ask questions about the time commitment, responsibilities, and any training that may be required. This will help you determine if the position is a good fit for you. By aligning your skills and interests with an organization's needs, you can ensure a fulfilling and impactful volunteer experience.

There are numerous volunteer opportunities to explore, catering to a wide range of interests. Mentoring and tutoring programs are an excellent choice if you enjoy working with people and have a passion for teaching. These programs allow you to share your knowledge and experience with others, providing them with guidance and support. Environmental conservation projects offer a chance to work outdoors and contribute to preserving our natural world. Whether planting trees, cleaning up parks, or participating in wildlife monitoring, these activities can be both physically rewarding and mentally rejuvenating.

. . .

Volunteering at hospitals and care facilities provides an opportunity to offer comfort and companionship to those in need. Many hospitals have programs in which volunteers assist with administrative tasks, visit patients, or help organize activities. This kind of volunteering can be incredibly fulfilling, as it allows you to directly and immediately impact someone's life. Participating in local charity events is another way to get involved. These events often require volunteer roles, such as event planning, fundraising, and on-the-day support. By helping out, you contribute to the success of the event and the cause it supports.

Consider the story of Sarah, a retiree who found a new purpose through mentoring. Sarah had a background in education and missed her interactions with students. She decided to volunteer with a local mentoring program for at-risk youth. Through her guidance and support, Sarah helped her mentee improve academically and develop essential life skills. The bond they formed was incredibly meaningful, providing Sarah with a renewed sense of purpose and fulfillment.

. . .

Then there's Paul, who made a significant difference through environmental conservation. After retiring, Paul wanted to spend more time outdoors and contribute to preserving the environment. He joined a local conservation group that focused on restoring natural habitats. Paul participated in tree planting, invasive species removal, and educational outreach. His efforts not only improved the local ecosystem but also connected him with a community of like-minded individuals. Paul's involvement in conservation work brought him immense satisfaction and a sense of accomplishment.

Volunteering offers a path to a more fulfilling and connected retirement. It enables you to use your skills and passions to impact the community while enriching your life. By assessing your interests, researching opportunities, and reaching out to organizations, you can find the perfect volunteer position. The possibilities are endless, whether it's mentoring, environmental work, or helping at a hospital. The stories of Sarah and Paul illustrate the profound impact volunteering can have, both on the community and on you.

3

TRAVEL AND ADVENTURE

"Because in the end, you won't remember the time you spent working in the office or mowing your lawn. Climb that goddamn mountain." — Jack Kerouac

Retirement is a time for rediscovery and exploration when the world becomes your playground. Imagine the open road calling your name, the thrill of immersing yourself in new cultures, the satisfaction of giving back to communities across the globe, or waking up in a new port every morning. This chapter will guide you through some of the most exhilarating and enriching travel experiences: those that offer the chance for adventure and opportunities to make lifelong friends, sharpen your mind, and ignite new passions.

Whether you're dreaming of leisurely road trips, adrenaline-pumping adventures, or transformative volunteer vacations, this section will inspire you to embrace the boundless opportunities retirement brings. Get ready to pack your bags and dive headfirst into the wonders of the world—because the adventure is just beginning.

Traveling on the Open Road

Picture the open road stretching out before you, a sense of freedom and possibility filling the air as you drive with the windows down and the wind in your hair. This is the allure of road trips, a travel option that offers flexibility, affordability, and the chance to explore at your own pace. For retirees, road trips can be a perfect way to rediscover the joy of travel without the hassle and cost of air travel. You can avoid long security lines, cramped airplane seats, and the stress of airports. Instead, you can stop whenever you want, explore hidden gems, and soak in scenic routes you otherwise might have missed.

. . .

Road trips allow you to travel on a flexible schedule. Unlike flights or train journeys, you're not bound by timetables on the open road. If you find a charming small town or a breathtaking view, you can take your time to explore. This flexibility means you can plan your trip based on your interests and energy levels, making it as leisurely or as packed with activities as you like. Plus, the cost savings are significant. Driving is generally cheaper than flying, especially if you bring your own snacks and drinks, avoiding expensive restaurant food. With road trips, you also have the option of staying in budget-friendly accommodations, further reducing costs.

When planning a budget-friendly road trip, there are several strategies to keep costs down while maximizing enjoyment. Using apps like Airbnb and Booking.com can help you find affordable accommodations. These platforms often offer discounts and deals, and you can read reviews to ensure you're getting good value for your money. Another tip is to pack essentials like snacks, water, and a first-aid kit. This not only saves money but also makes your journey more comfortable. Planning your route to include free or low-cost attractions can also be a great way to keep expenses in check. National parks, historical sites, and scenic drives often have minimal entrance fees and provide rich experiences.

There are many types of road trips to consider, each offering unique experiences. In the USA, coastal drives like the Pacific Coast Highway provide stunning ocean views and numerous opportunities to stop and explore beaches, lighthouses, and quaint seaside towns. National park tours, like those to Yellowstone or the Grand Canyon, offer breathtaking natural beauty and a chance to reconnect with nature. These trips can be particularly rewarding if you enjoy hiking, watching wildlife, or simply soaking in the majesty of the great outdoors. Historical routes, such as Route 66, take you through towns and landmarks rich in history and nostalgia. This type of trip can be an excellent way to learn about the past while enjoying the present.

Consider the story of George and Martha, who decided to tour the national parks in their RV. They mapped a route through Yellowstone, the Grand Canyon, and several other parks. With their home on wheels, they could stay as long as they liked at each destination. They hiked scenic trails, watched geysers erupt, and even spotted a grizzly bear. The experience was affordable and brought them closer together as they shared new adventures each day. For George and Martha, the road trip was a series of unforgettable moments that enriched their retirement.

Another inspiring example is Kathleen, who spent a summer exploring small-town America. She avoided the interstates and took back roads through picturesque towns and rural landscapes. Kathleen visited local diners, antique shops, and historical museums, experiencing the charm and hospitality of each community. She found joy in the simplicity of her journey, meeting new people and learning about the history and culture of each place she visited. Kathleen's road trip was a testament to the magic of slowing down and savoring the journey rather than rushing to the destination.

Road trips can be a fantastic way to maximize your retirement. They offer the freedom to explore at your own pace, discover hidden gems, and create lasting memories. Whether you're drawn to the coast, national parks, or historical routes, there's a road trip that can turn your travel dreams into reality. So, pack your bags, plan your path, and hit the open road. Your adventure awaits.

Exploring International Volunteer Vacations

Think about combining your love for travel with the opportunity to make a meaningful difference. This is the essence of volunteer vacations, where you explore new cultures while giving back to the communities you visit. These trips offer a unique blend of adventure and altruism, allowing you to experience the local way of life in a way that typical tourism cannot. By participating in volunteer projects, you build connections with local communities, gaining insights into their daily lives and challenges. This deepens your travel experience and provides a sense of fulfillment and purpose that comes from knowing your efforts are making a positive impact.

To find reputable volunteer vacation programs, look at organizations specializing in volunteer travel. Websites like Volunteer HQ and Projects Abroad offer a variety of programs tailored to different interests and skills. These platforms provide detailed information about each project, including the type of work involved, the duration, and the location. Reading reviews and testimonials from past volunteers can give you a better understanding of what to expect and help you choose a program that aligns with your goals. It's also important to consider how your skills and interests match the project's needs. For example, if you have a background in education, you may find teaching English in rural schools a fulfilling experience. Alternatively, if you are passionate about wildlife conservation, there are projects focused on protecting endangered species and preserving natural habitats.

Volunteer projects come in many forms, catering to various interests and skills. As mentioned above, teaching English in rural schools is popular, allowing you to share your knowledge and help students improve their language skills. This experience benefits the students and gives you a deeper understanding of the local educational system and culture. Wildlife conservation projects offer the chance to work closely with animals and contribute to preserving biodiversity. Whether it's protecting sea turtles on a beach or monitoring wildlife in a national park, these projects can be incredibly rewarding for nature lovers. Community development initiatives are another option, involving activities like building infrastructure, supporting healthcare services, or promoting sustainable practices. These projects address critical needs and can have a lasting impact on the community.

Consider the story of Martha, a retiree who decided to teach English in a remote village. Martha had always been passionate about education and wanted to make a difference in the lives of children. She found a program through Volunteer HQ that placed her in a small village with limited access to quality education. Martha spent several months teaching English to eager students, using creative methods to engage them and make learning fun. The experience was transformative for both Martha and her students. She gained a deeper appreciation for the local culture and formed lasting bonds with the children and their families. The students, in turn, improved their language skills, opening up new opportunities for their future.

Another inspiring example is provided by Tom and Linda, a couple who participated in an

African wildlife conservation project. They found a program through Projects Abroad that focused on protecting endangered rhinos in a national park. Tom and Linda spent their days tracking rhinos, collecting data, and assisting with anti-poaching efforts. The work was physically demanding but incredibly rewarding. They witnessed the beauty of the African landscape and the majesty of its wildlife, all while contributing to a vital cause. The experience brought them closer together and gave them a sense of fulfillment they had rarely felt before. Tom and Linda returned home with a newfound appreciation for conservation efforts and a determination to continue supporting these initiatives.

Volunteer vacations offer a unique way to travel, combining adventure with meaningful service. They allow you to immerse yourself in new cultures, build connections with local communities, and gain a sense of fulfillment and purpose. By researching reputable programs, aligning your skills with project needs, and choosing a volunteer opportunity that resonates with you, you can create an enriching and impactful travel experience. Whether teaching English, participating in wildlife conservation, or assisting with community development, the memories and connections you make will last a lifetime.

Group Travel: Tours and Cruises

Can you imagine this? You are stepping onto a cruise ship, greeted by friendly staff, knowing that everything is taken care of for the next week. This is the beauty of group travel for retirees. Tours and cruises offer convenience and safety that's hard to beat. With pre-planned itineraries, you can enjoy hassle-free travel without worrying about the details. Meals, accommodations, and activities are all arranged, allowing you to focus on the experience rather than the logistics. This kind of travel is not only stress-free but also provides numerous opportunities to meet and socialize with other travelers. You could find yourself making new friends over dinner or sharing stories during a guided tour. The shared experiences often create lasting bonds, adding a social dimension to your travels.

When choosing the right group travel experience, it's essential to consider a few key factors. Start by researching travel companies specializing in senior tours, such as Road Scholar or ElderTreks. These companies understand the needs and preferences of older travelers and often offer tailored experiences. Look into the length and pace of the trip. Some tours are fast-paced, covering many sites in a short time, while others are more leisurely, allowing you to savor each destination. Choose a pace that matches your energy levels and interests. It's also wise to look for packages that include meals, accommodations, and activities. This not only simplifies planning but can also be more cost-effective. Reading reviews and testimonials can provide insights into the tour's quality and previous travelers' experiences.

There are various types of group travel experiences to consider, each offering unique adventures. European river cruises are a popular choice, combining the charm of river travel with the opportunity to explore historic cities and picturesque villages. Imagine gliding down the Rhine, stopping to visit castles, vineyards, and bustling markets. These cruises often include guided tours, providing expert knowledge about the history and culture of each destination. Cultural tours of Asia offer another fascinating option. Explore the temples of Kyoto, the bustling streets of Bangkok, or the serene landscapes of Bali. These tours immerse you in the local culture with activities like cooking classes, traditional performances, and visits to local artisans. Adventure tours in South America provide a more dynamic experience. From hiking in Patagonia to exploring the Amazon rainforest, these tours cater to those who seek excitement and natural beauty.

Consider the story of Helen, a retiree who explored European cities on a river cruise. Helen had always dreamed of visiting Europe but was unsure where to start. She chose a river cruise that took her through several countries, including Germany, Austria, and Hungary. Each day brought new adventures, from touring medieval castles to sampling local delicacies at bustling markets. Helen appreciated the convenience of having everything organized, allowing her to enjoy the experience fully. She also made lasting friendships with fellow travelers, sharing meals and stories along the way. The cruise provided Helen with a rich and fulfilling travel experience, combining relaxation, exploration, and social connection.

Or take the example of John and Mary, a couple who joined a group tour of the historical sites of Japan. They had always been fascinated by Japanese culture and wanted to see it firsthand. The tour took them to iconic landmarks like the temples of Kyoto, the bustling streets of Tokyo, and the peaceful gardens of Nara. They participated in a traditional tea ceremony, learned about the art of calligraphy, and even tried making sushi. The guided tours provided deep insights into the history and traditions of each place they visited. John and Mary also enjoyed the camaraderie of their fellow travelers, sharing their excitement and curiosity. The tour fulfilled their travel dreams and enriched their understanding of a culture they had long admired.

Group travel offers numerous benefits, from convenience and safety to social opportunities and expert knowledge. Whether you choose a leisurely river cruise, an immersive cultural tour, or an adventurous trek, the experiences and connections you make will add depth and joy to your retirement years.

Adventure Travel for the Thrill-Seeker

Imagine standing on the edge of a cliff, the wind whipping around you as you take in a panoramic view of the mountains. Adventure travel can provide this kind of excitement, offering physical and mental challenges that push you out of your comfort zone and into a world filled with adrenaline and discovery. For retirees, embracing adventure travel can lead to personal growth and a renewed sense of vitality. It means overcoming fears, testing your limits, and experiencing the thrill of adventure in some of the most beautiful and remote destinations on Earth.

Choosing activities that match your fitness level and interests is crucial when planning an adventure trip. Whether you're interested in hiking the Inca Trail to Machu Picchu or scuba diving in the Great Barrier Reef, the key is finding something that excites you while being within your physical capabilities. Consulting with a doctor before undertaking physically demanding trips is a wise step to ensure you're ready for the adventure. Packing essential gear and clothing tailored to your specific activity is also important. Sturdy boots, weather-appropriate clothing, and a reliable backpack are must-haves for hiking. For scuba diving, ensure you have the right wetsuit, fins, and diving mask. Preparation is critical to enjoying your adventure safely and comfortably.

. . .

Adventure travel experiences come in many forms, catering to different levels of thrill-seeking. For example, hiking and trekking in the mountains offer a blend of physical exertion and breathtaking scenery. Imagine trekking through the Alps, where every turn reveals a new vista, or making your way along the ancient paths of the Inca Trail, culminating in the awe-inspiring sight of Machu Picchu. These hikes challenge your body and reward you with unparalleled views and a sense of accomplishment.

Scuba diving and snorkeling in exotic locations such as the Maldives or the Great Barrier Reef allow you to explore underwater worlds teeming with life. The thrill of diving beneath the waves and encountering colorful fish, coral reefs, and perhaps even a sea turtle or two, is an unforgettable experience. For those who prefer land-based adventures, wildlife safaris in Africa offer the excitement of seeing majestic animals in their natural habitats. Whether it's tracking lions in the Serengeti or observing elephants in Botswana, safaris provide a unique blend of adventure and education.

. . .

Consider Margaret, who decided to hike the Inca Trail to Machu Picchu. Margaret had always been fascinated by the history and mystery of the ancient Incan city but was unsure if she could handle the physical demands of the trek. She trained for months, gradually increasing her stamina and strength. When the day finally came, Margaret set off with a group of fellow adventurers, each step taking her closer to her goal. The trail was challenging, with steep climbs and rugged terrain, but the camaraderie of her group and the stunning landscapes kept her going. Reaching Machu Picchu at sunrise, Margaret felt a profound sense of accomplishment and awe. The journey tested her limits and proved that she was capable of more than she had ever imagined.

Another inspiring example is Paul, a retiree who went on a safari in Kenya. Paul had always dreamed of seeing Africa's wildlife up close but was hesitant about the logistics and safety. After researching reputable safari companies and consulting with his doctor, he decided to take the plunge. The safari exceeded his expectations. Each day brought new adventures, from watching a pride of lions lounging in the sun to witnessing the great migration of wildebeest across the

Serengeti. The experience was thrilling and deeply educational, offering insights into the delicate balance of Africa's ecosystems and the importance of conservation efforts. Paul returned home with a newfound appreciation for wildlife and a treasure trove of memories.

Adventure travel offers retirees the chance to challenge themselves, experience new thrills, and explore unspoiled destinations. Whether hiking, diving, or going on safari, each adventure provides unique opportunities for personal growth and unforgettable experiences. So, lace up those hiking boots, pack your gear, and get ready for the adventure of a lifetime.

Cultural Immersion Trips

Can you imagine waking up to the sound of roosters crowing in a rural village, stepping outside to see the sun rising over terraced fields, and sipping a cup of locally brewed coffee as the village comes to life? If so, cultural immersion trips might be for you. These deeply enriching experiences allow you to live like a local and truly understand a different way of life. These trips go beyond typical tourism, providing firsthand opportunities to learn about traditions, customs, and history. By immersing yourself in another culture, you build cross-cultural understanding and empathy, forming connections that go far beyond surface-level interactions.

Planning a cultural immersion trip requires thoughtful consideration and research. Start by selecting destinations that offer rich cultural experiences and are known for their hospitality. Homestays and cultural exchange programs are excellent options. They place you in the heart of the community, living with local families and participating in their daily routines. This type of stay provides a unique perspective on everyday life and fosters genuine connections with your hosts. Participating in cooking classes, language courses, or attending local festivals can further enhance your experience. These activities allow you to engage with the culture on a deeper level, learning skills and traditions that are integral to the local way of life. Researching cultural norms and etiquette beforehand is essential. Understanding and respecting these norms will enrich your experience and demonstrate your respect for the host culture.

. . .

There are various types of cultural immersion experiences to consider, each offering unique insights. Staying with a host family in a rural village can provide a profound understanding of community life and traditional practices. Imagine learning to weave intricate patterns on a loom—a skill passed down through generations—or helping your host family prepare a traditional meal using ingredients from their garden. Participating in traditional craft workshops, such as pottery or weaving, allows you to learn directly from artisans who have honed their skills over a lifetime. These workshops not only teach you new skills but also give you a deeper appreciation for the artistry and effort involved in traditional crafts. Attending local festivals and celebrations can be another highlight. These events often showcase the best of local culture, with music, dance, food, and rituals that have been practiced for centuries.

Consider the story of Deborah, who stayed with a host family in Japan. Deborah had always been fascinated by Japanese culture and wanted to experience it beyond tourist attractions. She found a homestay program placing her with a small village family. During her stay, Deborah participated in tea ceremonies, learned the art of calligraphy, and even joined the family in their daily chores, such as rice planting. The experience was transformative, providing Deborah with a deep appreciation for Japanese customs and a sense of belonging within the community. The bonds she formed with her host family were genuine and lasting, offering her a home away from home.

Another heartwarming example is Michael, a retiree who traveled to Italy to learn traditional cooking. Michael was passionate about cooking and wanted to immerse himself in Italian culinary traditions. He enrolled in a cooking class in a small Tuscan village, where he learned to make pasta, sauces, and desserts from scratch. The class was held in a rustic farmhouse, and each day, Michael and his classmates would gather fresh ingredients from the local market and the farm's garden. The hands-on experience, combined with the stories shared by the local chefs, provided Michael with a deep understanding of and love for Italian cuisine. The friendships he formed with his classmates and the locals enriched his travel experience, making it much more than just a cooking class.

. . .

Cultural immersion trips offer retirees a unique way to travel, providing opportunities to live like a local, learn about traditions, and build meaningful connections. Whether you stay with a host family, participate in traditional craft workshops, or attend local festivals, these experiences can profoundly transform your understanding of different cultures and enrich your life. Deborah and Michael's stories illustrate the joys and benefits of cultural immersion, showing that these trips can lead to lasting memories and connections that go far beyond typical tourism.

Travel and adventure can transform your retirement into a period of exploration and growth. From budget-friendly road trips to cultural immersion, each experience uniquely enriches your life. As you look ahead, remember that the world is full of opportunities waiting to be discovered. In the next chapter, we'll explore creative and artistic pursuits that can add even more joy and fulfillment to your retirement.

4

CREATIVE AND ARTISTIC PURSUITS

"Retirement, a time to enjoy all the things you never had time to do when you worked."

— CATHERINE PULSIFER

Think about standing in front of a blank canvas, brush in hand, ready to bring your imagination to life. Does this appeal to you? This is the magic of painting and drawing—a world where creativity knows no bounds, and every stroke tells a story. For many retirees, taking up art can be a wonderful way to explore new passions, express emotions, and find joy in the simple act of creating. Whether you've dabbled in art before or are a complete novice, this chapter will guide you through the basics and help you discover the artist within.

Painting and Drawing for Beginners

Starting your journey into painting and drawing can be both exciting and a bit intimidating. But worry not; the basics are easier to grasp than you might think. Begin with basic drawing techniques like contour drawing and shading. Contour drawing involves sketching the outline of a subject, focusing on capturing its shape and proportions. It's a great way to train your eye and improve hand-eye coordination. Shading, on the other hand, adds depth and dimension to your drawings. By varying the pressure on your pencil, you can create gradients that give your work a more realistic look.

Next, let's dive into the world of painting mediums. Watercolor, acrylic, and oil are the three most popular types you might encounter. Watercolors are known for their light, translucent quality and are perfect for those who enjoy a more fluid, spontaneous approach. Acrylics dry quickly and offer a vibrant range of colors, making them ideal for beginners who want immediate results. Oils, with their rich, buttery texture, allow for blending and layering, but they do take longer to dry and require more patience.

Before you start, gather some essential supplies. For drawing, you'll need good-quality pencils, erasers, and paper. A sketchbook is a great investment, providing you with a dedicated space to practice and experiment. For painting, stock up on brushes of various sizes, a palette for mixing colors, and either canvas or watercolor paper, depending on your chosen medium. Don't forget a smock or old shirt to protect your clothes—painting can get messy!

Now that you have your supplies, it's time for some hands-on practice. Begin by drawing basic shapes and still-life compositions. Set up a simple arrangement of objects like a mug, a fruit bowl, or a vase. Focus on capturing their shapes, proportions, and the way light and shadow play on their surfaces. Once you feel comfortable with drawing, move on to simple painting projects. Try your hand at landscapes, starting with broad strokes to outline the sky, hills, and trees. Experiment with abstract art by letting your emotions guide your brush, creating patterns and textures that speak to you. Techniques like blending colors and creating textures can add depth to your paintings. Mix colors directly on the canvas or use sponges and palette knives to achieve different effects.

Encouraging experimentation and personal expression is key to finding your unique style. Don't be afraid to try different styles and techniques until you find what resonates with you. Keep a sketchbook handy for daily practice and jotting down ideas. Sketching regularly not only improves your skills but also keeps your creative juices flowing. Joining local art classes or groups can provide support and inspiration. These communities offer a space to share your work, receive constructive feedback, and learn from others. Plus, they can be a lot of fun!

Consider Betty, a retiree who started with basic drawing and gradually progressed to exhibiting her work. Betty began by sketching simple still-life compositions in her kitchen. She found it relaxing and soon moved on to painting with watercolors. Her initial attempts were modest, but she persevered, taking classes at a local community center.

Over time, her confidence and skills grew. Betty's vibrant landscapes and delicate floral paintings caught the attention of a local gallery, and she was invited to exhibit her work. For Betty, what began as a hobby turned into a fulfilling second career.

Then there's Tim, who found relaxation and joy in watercolor painting. Tim had never considered himself artistic but decided to give it a try after retiring. He started with online tutorials, learning the basics of watercolor techniques. The process of blending colors and watching his paintings come to life was incredibly soothing. Tim soon realized that painting was more than a pastime; it was a way to unwind and express his emotions. He now spends his afternoons painting by the window, capturing the beauty of the changing seasons. Tim's journey shows that art can be both a creative outlet and a source of inner peace.

Writing Your Memoirs or a Novel

Imagine sitting at your desk, a blank page before you, ready to fill it with the stories of your life or the worlds created by your imagination. Writing a memoir or a novel can be a profoundly therapeutic and fulfilling endeavor. It offers a chance to reflect on your history, capturing the moments that have shaped you. By putting your experiences into words, you preserve them for future generations. This act of storytelling serves as a legacy and helps you make sense of your journey. Writing also allows for creative expression, letting your imagination take flight as you develop characters, plots, and settings. Moreover, writing enhances cognitive skills and mental clarity, keeping your mind active and engaged.

Getting started with writing may seem daunting, but breaking it down into manageable steps can make it more approachable. Begin by creating an outline. Consider the key events and themes you want to explore for a memoir. Organize these into a rough timeline or thematic structure. For a novel, sketch out your main characters, their motivations, and the plot's arc. Setting a writing schedule is important. Dedicate a specific time each day or week to write, even if it's just for thirty minutes. Consistency is critical to making progress. When it comes to drafting, don't worry about perfection. Focus on getting your thoughts down on paper; you can always revise later.

. . .

Developing characters and a plot for a novel requires thoughtful consideration. Characters should be multidimensional, with strengths, weaknesses, and motivations that drive the story forward. Think about their backgrounds, personalities, and relationships. The plot should have a clear beginning, middle, and end, with conflicts and resolutions that keep readers engaged. For memoirs, structuring and organizing your stories by themes or timelines can help create a cohesive narrative. Focus on a particular period or explore themes like family, career, or personal growth.

Different writing techniques and styles can help you find your voice. First-person narrative offers an intimate perspective, letting readers see the world through your eyes. The third-person narrative provides a broader view, allowing you to explore multiple characters and viewpoints. Using descriptive language can bring your stories to life, painting vivid pictures in the reader's mind. Dialogue can add depth to your characters and make interactions feel genuine. Incorporating personal anecdotes and reflections can also enrich your memoir, providing insights into your thoughts and feelings during crucial moments.

. . .

Consider the story of Alice, who published her memoirs in a local press. Alice had kept journals throughout her life, capturing her experiences and reflections. When she retired, she decided to compile these into memoirs. She created an outline based on the major phases of her life, from childhood to retirement. Alice set a daily writing schedule and gradually filled in the details, drawing from her journals and adding new reflections. Her memoirs were a heartfelt and authentic account of her life's journey. The local press published her work, and Alice's story resonated with many readers, providing them with inspiration and insights.

Another inspiring example is Robert, a retiree who wrote a novel and self-published it online. Robert had always been an avid reader and dreamed of writing a book. He developed a plot centered around a historical mystery and created detailed character sketches. Setting a strict writing schedule, Robert dedicated himself to writing every morning. He experimented with different techniques, finding that a third-person narrative suited his story best. After finishing his manuscript, Robert hired an editor to thoroughly review it and catch any edits he might have overlooked. He then decided to self-publish online. His novel gained a following, and Robert found immense satisfaction in sharing his creative work with the world.

Crafting with Recycled Materials

Can you imagine turning everyday household items into beautiful pieces of art? Crafting with recycled materials is not only a creative outlet but also a step toward promoting sustainability and environmental consciousness. By repurposing items that would otherwise end up in a landfill, you contribute to reducing waste and making the world a greener place. This art form encourages creativity and resourcefulness, pushing you to see the potential in what others might consider trash. Plus, it's a budget-friendly way to indulge in your artistic passions, saving money on traditional art supplies.

There are countless project ideas to explore when it comes to recycled crafts. You can start by creating sculptures from household items. For instance, gather bottle caps, old CDs, and even tin cans to construct whimsical figures or abstract forms. The process is simple: sketch a design, assemble your materials, and use hot glue or other adhesives to bring your creation to life. Making jewelry from recycled materials is another exciting avenue. Paper beads crafted from old magazines or fabric scraps can be turned into unique necklaces and bracelets. Cut the paper or fabric into strips, roll them tightly, and secure them with glue. String them together using elastic or wire to complete your piece. Home decor items are also a fantastic way to incorporate recycled materials into your crafts. Old glass bottles can be transformed into vases by painting or wrapping them with twine, and cardboard can be cut and painted to create striking wall art.

Participating in community recycling and crafting events can add a social dimension to your creative pursuits. Local recycling workshops and craft fairs often provide a platform to learn new techniques and share your creations with others. These events are not only educational but also a great way to meet like-minded individuals who share your passion for sustainability. Community art projects and installations frequently seek volunteers to contribute their skills, offering a collaborative environment to work on larger pieces that can be displayed publicly. Online crafting communities and challenges are another excellent resource. Platforms like Pinterest and Facebook groups allow you to share your projects, get feedback, and find inspiration from others worldwide.

Here's the story of Pamela, a retiree who created a stunning garden sculpture from discarded items. Pamela had always been an avid gardener and wanted to add unique decorations to her outdoor space. She collected old metal tools, broken pottery, and even bicycle parts. With some creativity and welding skills, Pamela transformed these materials into a whimsical garden statue that became the centerpiece of her yard. Her project beautified her garden and sparked conversations with neighbors, many of whom were inspired to start their own recycled art projects.

Then there's Bob, who turned his passion for recycled crafts into a small business. Bob started by making decorative items from old wine corks, such as coasters and picture frames. Encouraged by the positive feedback from friends and family, he decided to expand his repertoire. Bob began crafting birdhouses from old wooden pallets and jewelry from discarded electronics. He set up a booth at local craft fairs and eventually opened an online shop. Bob's business not only provided him with a steady income in retirement but also gave him a sense of purpose and fulfillment. His story demonstrates the potential of recycled crafts to grow from a simple hobby into a successful venture.

Crafting with recycled materials offers a fulfilling and sustainable way to express your creativity. It allows you to see the beauty and potential in everyday items, transforming them into works of art. The possibilities are endless, whether you're making sculptures, jewelry, or home decor. Engaging in community events and sharing your creations online can further enrich your crafting experience, providing opportunities for social interaction and collaboration. So, gather those old bottle caps, CDs, and fabric scraps and create something beautiful and unique. The joy of crafting is in the process, the creativity, and the positive impact on the environment.

Photography: Capturing Life's Moments

Envision holding a camera, ready to capture the world around you. Photography offers a unique way to see and document life's precious moments. This creative pursuit enhances your observation skills, making you more attuned to the details that often go unnoticed. The way light falls on a leaf, the expression on a loved one's face, or the vibrant colors of a sunset—photography helps you preserve these fleeting moments, turning them into lasting memories. It also allows you to explore artistic expression through composition and lighting, creating images that tell a story or evoke emotions.

Starting with photography can feel overwhelming, but selecting the right equipment makes it easier. Choose a camera that meets your needs and budget. DSLRs and mirrorless cameras offer more control and higher-quality images, while compact cameras are user-friendly and portable. Essential accessories include a sturdy tripod to keep your shots steady and a selection of lenses if you opt for a camera with interchangeable lenses. A wide-angle lens is great for landscapes, while a macro lens lets you capture intricate details up close.

Understanding camera settings is crucial for taking great photos. Aperture, shutter speed, and

ISO are the three main elements of exposure. The aperture controls the amount of light entering the lens and affects the depth of field. Shutter speed determines how long the camera's sensor is exposed to light, influencing motion blur. ISO adjusts the camera's sensitivity to light, which can help in low-light conditions but may introduce noise at higher settings. Practice using these settings in manual mode to see how they affect your images.

Basic composition techniques can elevate your photography. The rule of thirds is a simple yet effective guideline. Imagine dividing your frame into a grid of nine equal parts. Place key elements along these lines or at their intersections to create a balanced and engaging image. Leading lines, such as roads or rivers, guide the viewer's eye through the photo and add depth. Framing subjects with natural elements like trees or doorways can also create a more compelling composition.

Photography offers various genres to explore, catering to different interests. Landscape photography captures the beauty of nature, from majestic mountains to serene beaches. It requires patience and an eye for lighting and weather conditions. Portrait photography focuses on people, capturing their expressions and personalities. Whether it's a candid shot or a posed portrait, this genre allows for deep emotional connection. Macro photography delves into the tiny world of small subjects, revealing details that are often invisible to the naked eye. Flowers, insects, and textures become fascinating subjects when viewed up close.

Consider the story of Sharon, who found joy in nature photography. After retiring, she started walking in her local park with her camera. Sharon's keen eye for detail and patience paid off as she captured stunning images of birds, flowers, and landscapes. Her work soon caught the attention of a local art gallery, and she was invited to exhibit her photographs. The experience boosted her confidence and gave her a new sense of purpose. Today, Sharon's photos are celebrated for their beauty and unique perspective.

Another example is Robert, a retiree who documented his travels through photography. Robert loved to explore new places, and his camera became his constant companion. He captured the bustling streets of cities, the tranquility of remote villages, and the diverse cultures he encountered. His photographs preserved his travel memories and allowed him to share his experiences with family and friends. Robert's photo albums became a visual diary of his adventures, filled with stories and emotions that words alone couldn't convey.

Photography is a rewarding and enriching hobby that lets you capture and share the world's beauty. Whether you're interested in landscapes, portraits, or macro photography, the skills you develop and the moments you capture will bring lasting joy and fulfillment. So, pick up your camera, venture out, and capture life's moments.

Music and Dance: Learning an Instrument or Dance Style

Does this spark any interest in you? Imagine the joy of playing a beautiful melody on the piano or moving gracefully to the rhythm of a waltz. Learning music and dance can enhance your physical, mental, and emotional well-being. These activities are enjoyable and beneficial for improving cognitive function and memory. Studies have shown that playing an instrument engages multiple brain areas, enhancing neural connections and keeping your mind sharp. Similarly, learning dance routines require memorization and coordination, which can boost brain function.

When it comes to physical fitness, both music and dance offer excellent benefits. Playing an instrument like the guitar or piano requires fine motor skills, improving hand-eye coordination and dexterity. Dancing, whether it's ballroom or Zumba, provides a full-body workout. It boosts cardiovascular health, strengthens muscles, and enhances flexibility. The physical exertion involved in dancing also releases endorphins, elevating your mood and reducing stress. Additionally, both music and dance provide a sense of accomplishment and joy. Whether you master a challenging piece of music or learn a new dance move, the satisfaction of achieving something new can be deeply fulfilling.

Learning an instrument begins with choosing one that suits your interests and physical abilities. If you're drawn to the soothing sounds of strings, consider the guitar or violin. For something more rhythmic, the drums may be a good fit. Piano offers a versatile option, suitable for beginners and experts alike. Once you've selected an instrument, look for resources to help you learn. Online tutorials on platforms like YouTube can provide beginner-friendly lessons. Local music teachers can offer personalized instruction, tailoring lessons to your pace and skill level. Setting a practice schedule is essential. Dedicate a specific time each day or week to practice, and stay motivated by setting small, achievable goals.

Exploring different dance styles can open up a world of possibilities. Ballroom dancing, such as the waltz or tango, offers a graceful and structured form of dance that's perfect for social events. These dances emphasize posture, coordination, and elegant movements. Social dancing, like salsa or line dancing, brings a lively and energetic vibe. These styles are great for meeting new people and enjoying a fun, communal activity. If you're looking for a fitness-focused option, consider Zumba or jazzercise. These dance workouts combine aerobic exercise with upbeat music, making it a fun way to stay fit.

. . .

Ed is a retiree who learned to play the piano and joined a community band. Ed had always admired pianists but never had the time to learn. After retiring, he bought a keyboard and started with online tutorials. After diligent practice, he gradually improved his skills. Ed soon joined a local community band and met other music enthusiasts. The camaraderie and shared passion for music brought him immense joy and a sense of belonging. Ed's journey illustrates how learning an instrument can lead to new friendships and fulfilling experiences.

Then there's Janet, who became a regular at local dance classes. Janet had always loved dancing but never pursued it seriously. After retiring, she signed up for ballroom dance classes at a nearby studio. She quickly fell in love with the elegant movements and the social aspect of the classes. Janet made new friends and even participated in local dance competitions. The physical activity kept her fit, and the joy of dancing uplifted her spirits. Janet's experience shows that it's always possible to discover a passion for dance and enjoy its many benefits.

. . .

Learning music and dance can transform your retirement into a vibrant and fulfilling time. These activities offer numerous benefits, from improved cognitive and physical health to emotional well-being. Whether you play a new instrument or learn a dance style, the sense of accomplishment and joy you gain will enrich your life in countless ways. So, pick up that guitar, sit at that piano, or put on your dancing shoes. The world of music and dance awaits you.

Chapter 4 has explored various creative and artistic pursuits that can bring joy and fulfillment to your retirement. From painting and writing to crafting and photography, each activity offers unique benefits and opportunities for personal growth. As we move forward, let's delve into another exciting aspect of retirement: health and fitness.

5

HEALTH AND FITNESS

"Take care of your body. It's the only place you have to live."

— JIM ROHN

Wouldn't it be great to wake up each morning feeling energized and ready to take on the day, free from the aches and pains that can sometimes accompany aging? This is the promise of maintaining good health and fitness in retirement. As you step into this new chapter of life, focusing on your physical well-being can significantly enhance your quality of life, making everyday activities more enjoyable and fulfilling.

Health and fitness are not just about adding years to your life but life to your years. Regularly exercising and maintaining a balanced diet can boost your energy levels, improve your mood, and reduce the risk of chronic diseases.

Low-Impact Exercises for Joint Health

Low-impact exercises offer numerous benefits for joint health, making them an ideal choice for retirees. These exercises are designed to reduce stress on your joints, which is crucial for those who may experience joint pain or stiffness. By minimizing the impact on the joints, these exercises allow you to stay active without aggravating any existing issues. Additionally, low-impact exercises improve flexibility and range of motion, helping you move more freely and comfortably throughout the day. Strengthening the muscles around your joints provides added support, reducing the risk of injury and enhancing overall stability.

One of the most effective low-impact exercises is gentle stretching. Stretching helps maintain flexibility, which is essential for joint health. Start with simple stretches like reaching for your toes while seated or standing, gently twisting your torso to the left and right, and stretching your arms overhead. Hold each stretch for about twenty to thirty seconds, breathing deeply to relax your muscles. Chair exercises are another excellent option, especially if you have limited mobility. These exercises can be performed while seated, making them accessible and safe. Try lifting your legs one at a time, extending them straight out in front of you, or doing seated marches by lifting your knees alternately. Low-impact aerobics, such as walking or cycling on a stationary bike, provide cardiovascular benefits without putting undue strain on your joints. These activities help you maintain a healthy weight—which is crucial for joint health—and improve overall endurance.

Consistency and gradual progression are key to reaping the benefits of low-impact exercises. It's important to set a regular exercise schedule that you can stick to. Aim for at least thirty minutes of activity most days of the week. Starting slowly and gradually increasing the duration and intensity of your workouts can prevent overexertion and reduce the risk of injury. Listen to your body and avoid pushing yourself too hard. If you feel pain or discomfort, take a break and consult a healthcare professional if necessary. The goal is to find a balance that allows you to stay active while protecting your joints.

Consider Barbara, a retiree who improved her mobility through daily stretching routines. Barbara had always enjoyed an active lifestyle, but arthritis in her knees made it difficult for her to continue high-impact activities. She started incorporating gentle stretching exercises into her morning routine, focusing on her legs and lower back. Over time, she noticed significantly improved flexibility and reduced pain. Barbara's daily stretching routine allowed her to stay active and enjoy her favorite hobbies, like gardening and walking her dog, without discomfort.

Another inspiring example is Richard, who found relief from arthritis pain with chair exercises. Richard had struggled with joint pain for years, making it challenging for him to stay active. He discovered a series of chair exercises that targeted his arms, legs, and core, providing a full-body workout without the strain of traditional exercises. Richard began performing these exercises daily, gradually increasing the number of repetitions and adding light weights for resistance. The chair exercises helped alleviate his pain and improved his overall strength and balance, allowing him to move more confidently and enjoy life to the fullest.

Incorporating low-impact exercises into your daily routine can profoundly impact your joint health and overall well-being. Whether stretching, performing chair exercises, or engaging in low-impact aerobics, staying consistent and listening to your body is key. By doing so, you can enjoy the many benefits of staying active while protecting your joints and enhancing your quality of life.

Interactive Element: Sample Stretching Routine

1. **Seated Toe Touch:** Sit on the edge of a chair with your feet flat on the floor. Slowly reach for your toes, keeping your back straight. Hold for 20–30 seconds.
2. **Torso Twist:** Sit upright with your feet flat on the floor. Gently twist your torso to the left, placing your right hand on

the outside of your left thigh for support. Hold for 20–30 seconds. Repeat on the other side.
3. **Overhead Stretch:** Sit or stand with your feet shoulder-width apart. Raise your arms overhead and interlock your fingers. Gently stretch upwards, feeling the stretch in your back and shoulders. Hold for 20–30 seconds.
4. **Leg Extension:** Sit on a chair with your feet flat on the floor. Extend your right leg straight out in front of you, holding for 10 seconds. Lower your leg and repeat with your left leg. Perform 10 repetitions on each side.
5. **Seated Marches:** Sit upright with your feet flat on the floor. Lift your right knee toward your chest, then lower it. Repeat with your left knee. Perform 20 marches in total.

Integrating this sample routine into your daily schedule can enhance your flexibility, reduce joint pain, and improve overall mobility.

Yoga and Meditation for Mind-Body Balance

Yoga and meditation are more popular than ever. Imagine starting your day with gentle stretches and deep breaths, feeling your body wake up and your mind clear. Yoga and meditation offer this and so much more, enhancing your physical, mental, and emotional health. These practices can improve flexibility and strength, helping you move with ease and confidence. Yoga stretches and poses strengthen muscles, improve balance, and enhance your range of motion, making everyday tasks easier and reducing the risk of falls. Beyond the physical benefits, yoga and meditation are powerful tools for reducing stress and anxiety. Focusing on breath and mindfulness helps calm the mind, lowering stress levels and promoting inner peace. This mental clarity and focus can improve your overall well-being, making it easier to navigate the ups and downs of daily life.

Getting started with yoga is simpler than you might think. One of the first steps is choosing a suitable yoga style. Hatha yoga is an excellent option for beginners, focusing on basic poses and gentle stretches. Yin yoga emphasizes slow, deep stretches held for more extended periods, promoting relaxation and flexibility. Chair yoga offers modifications of traditional poses, making them accessible for those with balance issues or limited mobility. Once you've chosen a style, find a class that suits your needs. Many local yoga studios offer beginner classes, and online platforms like YouTube provide many free instructional videos. Essential yoga props can enhance your practice, providing support and comfort. A good-quality yoga mat offers a stable, non-slip surface. Blocks and straps can assist with poses, helping you achieve proper alignment and deepen stretches.

Meditation complements yoga beautifully, offering a way to cultivate mindfulness and mental calm. Starting with basic meditation techniques can make the practice approachable. Mindfulness meditation involves focusing on the present moment and observing your thoughts and sensations without judgment. Find a quiet, comfortable space to sit, close your eyes, and bring your attention to your breath. Notice the feeling of the breath entering and leaving your body, gently redirecting your focus whenever your mind wanders. Guided visualization is another effective technique. This involves listening to a recorded script that guides you through a series of calming images and scenarios. It can be beneficial for reducing anxiety and promoting relaxation. Breathing exercises like deep diaphragmatic breathing can also enhance your meditation practice. Sit comfortably and take slow, deep breaths, filling your lungs thoroughly and exhaling completely. This simple practice can quickly calm your nervous system and improve your focus.

Let's explore the story of Anne, a retiree who gained flexibility and strength through yoga. Anne had always been curious about yoga but never found the time to try it. After retiring, she joined a local Hatha yoga class. The gentle poses and stretches were accessible, and the instructor provided modifications to suit her abilities. Over time, Anne noticed a significant improvement in her flexibility and balance. She could reach higher, bend more efficiently, and feel more stable. The strength she gained from yoga also helped alleviate some of the aches and pains she had experienced, making her daily activities more enjoyable.

There's also Tom, who found inner peace with daily meditation. Tom had struggled with anxiety for years, and retirement brought new stressors as he adjusted to a different lifestyle. He decided to try mindfulness meditation, starting with just five minutes each morning. Tom found a quiet corner of his home, closed his eyes, and focused on his breath. The practice was challenging at first, but he persisted. Gradually, Tom increased his meditation sessions to twenty minutes. The impact on his mental health was profound. He felt calmer, more focused, and better equipped to handle stress. The inner peace meditation was transformative in Tom's life, enhancing his overall well-being.

Yoga and meditation offer a holistic approach to health, addressing both the body and mind. Incorporating these practices into your routine can improve your physical strength and flexibility, reduce stress and anxiety, and enhance your mental clarity and focus. Whether you're stretching on a yoga mat or sitting quietly in meditation, the benefits of these practices can enrich your retirement, helping you live a healthier, more balanced life.

Swimming and Water Aerobics

How does this sound—you are gliding through the water, feeling weightless and free from the stress on your joints. Swimming and water aerobics offer a full-body workout that is gentle on your body. These activities enhance cardiovascular health by increasing your heart rate without the strain of high-impact exercises. The resistance of the water helps improve muscle tone and strength, making your muscles work harder than they would on land. Additionally, the buoyancy of the water reduces joint pain and stiffness, providing a comfortable environment for exercise, especially if you have arthritis or other joint issues.

Getting started with swimming and water aerobics is easier than you may think. Start by locating community pools and aquatic centers in your area. Many facilities offer dedicated times for lap swimming, water aerobics classes, and even specialized programs for older adults. Signing up for water aerobics classes can provide structured exercise sessions led by experienced instructors. These classes often cater to different fitness levels, ensuring that you can participate regardless of your current physical condition. Choosing the right swimwear and accessories is also important. Look for comfortable, well-fitting swimsuits designed for active use, and consider wearing water shoes for added grip and stability. Goggles can help protect your eyes from chlorine, making your swimming experience more enjoyable.

Various types of water-based exercises suit different fitness levels and preferences. Lap swimming is a classic choice, allowing you to swim at your own pace while building cardiovascular endurance and muscle strength. Start with a few laps and gradually increase your distance as your fitness improves. Water walking and running are excellent low-impact options. These activities involve walking or jogging through the water, which provides resistance while reducing impact on your joints. Aqua Zumba combines the fun of dance with the benefits of water exercise. These energetic classes feature dance routines set to lively music, offering a fun and social way to stay fit.

Carol is a retiree who improved her fitness through regular swimming. Carol had always enjoyed swimming but struggled to maintain a consistent routine during her working years. After retiring, she committed to swimming three times a week at her local pool. Carol started with short sessions, gradually increasing her distance and intensity. Over time, she noticed significant improvements in her cardiovascular health, muscle tone, and overall energy levels. Swimming became a meditative experience for Carol, allowing her to clear her mind and enjoy the rhythmic flow of the water.

Larry is another inspiring example; he found joy in water aerobics classes. Larry had been struggling with joint pain and stiffness, making traditional exercise challenging. A friend recommended water aerobics, and Larry gave it a shot. He joined a class at his local aquatic center, where the supportive and social atmosphere quickly put him at ease. The instructor guided the class through exercises that targeted different muscle groups, all while keeping the movements gentle on the joints. Larry found the buoyancy of the water alleviated his pain, allowing him to move more freely and confidently. The camaraderie of the class added a social dimension to his workouts, making exercise something to look forward to.

Swimming and water aerobics offer a unique way to stay fit and healthy. They combine the benefits of a full-body workout with the gentle support of water. Whether swimming laps, walking through the water, or dancing in an Aqua Zumba class, these activities can enhance physical fitness while being kind to your joints. By incorporating swimming and water-based exercises into your routine, you can enjoy the physical, mental, and social benefits that come with staying active in the water.

Joining a Walking or Hiking Group

Walking and hiking offer a wonderful blend of physical and mental health benefits. These activities provide low-impact exercise, making them accessible to many people, regardless of age or fitness level. Walking regularly can improve cardiovascular health, helping to keep your heart strong and your blood pressure in check. The rhythmic movement and fresh air can also enhance your mood and reduce stress. It's hard to feel anxious when surrounded by nature or engaging in a lively conversation with a walking buddy. Additionally, joining a walking or hiking group offers the added bonus of social interaction. You'll meet new people, form friendships, and build a supportive community.

. . .

Finding and joining a walking or hiking group is usually easy. Start by checking local community centers and parks, as they often host walking clubs or can point you to existing groups. Online platforms like Meetup are also great resources. Search for walking or hiking groups in your area, and you'll probably find several options to choose from. Don't hesitate to ask friends and family for recommendations either; they may know of a group that would be a perfect fit for you. Once you find a group, contact the organizer to learn more about the group's schedule, route, and pace. This can help ensure that the group aligns with your interests and fitness level.

Walking and hiking come in many forms, catering to different interests and fitness levels. Urban walking tours offer a fantastic way to explore your city. These tours often focus on historical landmarks, architectural highlights, or even local food scenes. They provide a leisurely pace and plenty of opportunities to stop and learn. Nature hikes in local parks are another excellent option. These hikes allow you to immerse yourself in the beauty of nature, whether it's a forest trail, a lakeside path, or a mountain route. The varied terrain and natural surroundings can make each hike a unique adventure. For those looking for a more challenging experience, long-distance trail hiking offers an unparalleled sense of accomplishment. Trails like the Appalachian Trail or the Camino de Santiago provide opportunities for extended hikes, often spanning several days or even weeks. These trails are physically rewarding and offer a chance for deep reflection and personal growth.

Consider the story of Bill, a retiree who found a new passion for hiking. Bill had always enjoyed the outdoors but never considered hiking a regular activity. After retiring, he joined a local hiking group he found on Meetup. The group met every Saturday and explored different trails in the area. Bill quickly became hooked, discovering the joy of hiking through forests, up hills, and along rivers. The physical exercise improved his cardiovascular health, and the camaraderie of the group enriched his social life. Bill even started planning his own hiking trips, exploring new trails, and challenging himself to longer hikes.

Another inspiring example is Barbara, who built lasting friendships through a local walking group. After retiring, Barbara moved to a new city and was looking for ways to meet people. She joined a community walking club that met three times a week at a nearby park. The group welcomed her with open arms, and she quickly became a regular member. The walks were filled with lively conversations, shared experiences, and plenty of laughter. Barbara's fitness improved, and she felt more connected to her new community. The friendships she formed through the walking group became vital to her social life, providing support and companionship.

Walking and hiking offer a unique way to stay active and socially engaged. Exploring urban landscapes, enjoying nature trails, or tackling long-distance hikes can enhance your physical health and enrich your social life. So lace up your walking (or hiking) shoes, find a group that suits your interests, and start exploring the world one step at a time.

Pickleball for Seniors

Pickleball is a fast-growing sport that combines elements of tennis, badminton, and table tennis. Pickleball is played on a smaller court with a paddle and a perforated plastic ball. These unique aspects have made pickleball especially popular among seniors. The game is easy to learn, but its depth of strategy keeps players coming back for more.

Pickleball is an ideal sport for seniors for several reasons. First, it's a low-impact exercise that is more gentle on the joints while providing a great workout. The smaller court size reduces the required running, encouraging quick, controlled movements that are easier on the body. It's also a fantastic way to stay socially active and build a community.

I stumbled upon pickleball somewhat by chance. Not knowing much about the sport, I decided to search online for "pickleball courts near me" and see what it was all about. As a long-time squash player, I initially found the shorter paddle and lighter ball challenging. But once I adjusted, I quickly began to enjoy the game. What surprised me most was the strategy and teamwork involved. Unlike the intense solo focus of squash, pickleball requires you to think several steps ahead, collaborating closely with your partner to outmaneuver your opponents. This strategic element was unexpected but incredibly engaging.

While playing, I became absorbed in each rally, eagerly planning my next move. Beyond the game itself, I was amazed by the social benefits. Within weeks, I had developed meaningful relationships with my fellow players, who ranged from beginners to seasoned pros. This community aspect made me look forward to each session, not just for the game but for the camaraderie.

For those interested in trying pickleball, getting started is easy. The basic rules are simple, and you don't need much equipment—just a paddle, a ball, and comfortable athletic shoes. Many communities have local courts or clubs, and it's common to find beginner-friendly sessions. My advice is to simply take the plunge, as I did, and find a nearby court to join.

Playing pickleball provides numerous health benefits. It's a great cardiovascular workout that can improve heart health and increase endurance.

The quick, agile movements required help improve balance and coordination, which is especially important as we age. The mental strategy also keeps the brain sharp, adding cognitive benefits to the mix. Moreover, the emotional benefits are substantial; social interaction and friendly competition help reduce stress and promote overall well-being.

One of the greatest joys of pickleball is the community it creates. Whether playing casually or in a more competitive setting, the game fosters a welcoming environment where players encourage and support each other. In my experience, this sense of belonging and the friendships I've formed have been as rewarding as the physical exercise.

Pickleball has taught me that it's never too late to try something new. Whether you're a seasoned athlete or just looking for a fun way to stay active, pickleball offers something for everyone. It's more than just a game—it's a gateway to a healthier, more connected lifestyle. So grab a paddle and join in the fun. Like I did, you might find it becomes your new favorite pastime!

Nutrition Tips for Active Seniors

One of the best things about eating well is feeling vibrant and energetic every day, ready to enjoy all the activities you love. Proper nutrition can help make this a reality. A balanced diet is crucial for supporting both physical and mental health as you age. It provides the energy needed for daily activities, ensuring you remain active and engaged. A well-rounded diet also enhances immune function, helping you fend off illnesses and maintain overall well-being. Additionally, it supports muscle maintenance and bone health, which are vital for staying strong and mobile.

Incorporating a variety of fruits and vegetables into your meals is a great starting point for a healthy diet. These foods are rich in essential vitamins, minerals, and antioxidants that promote good health. Aim to fill half your plate with colorful fruits and vegetables at each meal. Choose lean proteins like chicken, fish, and legumes to support muscle health. Whole grains such as brown rice, quinoa, and whole wheat bread provide sustained energy and are high in fiber. Staying hydrated is equally important. Drink plenty of water throughout the day and limit processed foods high in sugar, salt, and unhealthy fats.

Seniors have specific dietary needs that should not be overlooked. Calcium and vitamin D are essential for bone health. Your bones can become more brittle as you age, increasing the risk of fractures. Incorporate calcium-rich foods like dairy products, leafy greens, and fortified cereals into your diet. Vitamin D, which aids calcium absorption, can be found in fortified foods and supplements. Protein is another critical nutrient for muscle maintenance. Include a variety of protein sources in your meals to ensure you're getting enough. Managing portion sizes and calorie intake is also essential. Overeating can lead to weight gain, while eating too little can result in nutrient deficiencies.

Consider the story of Emily, a retiree who adopted a plant-based diet and saw remarkable health improvements. Emily had always struggled with high cholesterol and wanted to make a change. She decided to switch to a plant-based diet, focusing on fruits, vegetables, whole grains, and legumes. Within a few months, Emily noticed significant improvements in her cholesterol levels and her overall energy. She felt more vibrant and even lost a few pounds. Emily's story is a testament to the power of dietary changes in improving health.

Another inspiring example is James, who learned to cook healthy meals after retiring. James had relied on takeout and pre-packaged meals for years, leading to weight gain and low energy levels. Determined to make a change, he started taking cooking classes at a local community center. James learned how to prepare nutritious meals using fresh ingredients. He began experimenting with new recipes and found joy in cooking. The changes in his diet led to weight loss, improved energy, and a greater sense of well-being. James's journey highlights the importance of learning to cook healthy meals and the positive impact it can have on your health.

Proper nutrition is the foundation of a healthy and active lifestyle. You can support your physical and mental health by focusing on a balanced diet rich in fruits, vegetables, lean proteins, and whole grains. Remember to pay attention to your specific dietary needs, such as increasing calcium and vitamin D intake for bone health and ensuring adequate protein for muscle maintenance. The stories of Emily and James illustrate how dietary changes can lead to significant health improvements, inspiring you to make healthier choices. Make sure you consult with your physician before making any significant changes to your diet.

Help Others Create a Bolder, Brighter, More Focused Version of Themselves

"If you look at what you have in life, you'll always have more. If you look at what you don't have in life, you'll never have enough." — Oprah Winfrey

Retirement is undoubtedly one of the major milestones in life. Similarly to a teen leaving home for the first time to attend college or a professional moving abroad to embark on anew work opportunity, seniors have a unique opportunity to reinvent themselves. They have a chance to spend time on their passions and set new goals, or better yet, revisit those they have set aside because making a living has been their number one priority for so many years.

I wrote this book because I realized that when you've been fully immersed in your career, and you suddenly exit the rat race, there can be a sense of curiosity about what to do with so much spare time. But who said you had to give yourself time enough to get bored? Thus far, you have discovered strategies for rediscovering yourself, hosting social gatherings, traveling, and getting back into great shape. All these activities will fill your days, so much that you'll be busier than ever! You have also seen how creative pursuits such as drawing, music and dance, or crafting have incredible mental health benefits, keeping you on your toes while being a proven form of stress relief! If you are excited about filling your diary with many of the experiences suggested, kindly take a brief pause and let other seniors know what they will find within these pages!

By leaving a review of this book on Amazon, you'll show new readers that every day is a chance to hone a new skill, feel healthier and stronger, and discover new things about themselves and the world.

It will only take a minute or two, but it could enlighten others on the opportunities that are finally within their reach!

Scan the QR code below

6

LIFELONG LEARNING AND EDUCATION

"The more I learn, the more I realize how much I don't know."

— ALBERT EINSTEIN

Imagine sitting at your kitchen table with a cup of coffee, opening your laptop, and diving into a course on ancient history from a prestigious university halfway across the world. The possibilities are endless, and the best part is that you can do it all from the comfort of your own home. Lifelong learning is not just a buzzword; it's a way to keep your mind sharp, stay engaged with the world, and continue growing intellectually. For retirees, online learning offers an incredibly flexible and diverse way to explore new interests, enhance skills, and even pursue passions that were once set aside.

Enrolling in Online Courses

Online learning platforms have revolutionized education, making it accessible to people of all ages. For retirees, the flexibility these platforms offer is a game-changer. You can learn at your own pace and convenience, fitting your studies around your daily routine rather than the other way around. Whether you're an early bird who likes to study in the morning or a night owl who prefers diving into lessons after dinner, online courses accommodate your schedule. This flexibility allows you to engage deeply with the material without the pressure of deadlines, making the learning experience more enjoyable and less stressful.

One of the significant benefits of online learning is access to courses from prestigious institutions. Platforms like Coursera, edX, and Udemy collaborate with top universities and industry leaders to offer classes in a wide range of subjects. These platforms provide user-friendly interfaces and a vast array of courses. You can take a course in digital marketing from the University of Illinois, learn mindfulness from Yale, or delve into computer science at MIT. These courses often feature interactive content, including video lectures, quizzes, and discussion forums, which enhance the learning experience. Engaging with interactive content and discussions helps solidify your understanding and allows you to connect with fellow learners from around the globe, fostering a sense of community even in a virtual setting.

Finding and enrolling in online courses is straightforward, but a few tips can help you choose the best options. Reading reviews and course descriptions can provide valuable insights into the course's quality and what to expect. Review previous students' ratings and feedback to gauge whether the course aligns with your interests and learning style. Many platforms also offer free or affordable course options, allowing you to explore subjects without a significant financial commitment. For instance, Coursera offers free audit options that allow you to access course materials, though you'll need to pay if you want a certificate.

. . .

The variety of subjects available in online courses is staggering, catering to nearly every interest imaginable. If personal development is your goal, consider mindfulness, public speaking, or creative writing courses. These subjects enhance your skills and contribute to your overall well-being. For those looking to update their professional skills, courses in digital marketing, project management, or even coding can be incredibly beneficial. These classes can help you stay current in your field or even transition into a new one. Academic subjects like history, psychology, or literature allow you to dive deep into areas you've always been curious about but never had the time to explore fully. The beauty of online learning is that there is always time to start something new!

Take the story of Helen, who completed a history course at a renowned university. Helen had always been fascinated by medieval history but never had the chance to study it formally. After retiring, she enrolled in a course on Coursera offered by the University of London. The course included video lectures, readings, and interactive discussions with fellow students. Helen found the material captivating and the discussions enriching. By the end of the course, she felt a deep sense of accomplishment and a renewed passion for history. This experience broadened her knowledge and connected her with a global community of learners who shared her interests.

After retirement, Robert learned web design through an online platform. Robert had always been intrigued by technology but considered himself a computer novice. He decided to enroll in a web design course on Udemy. The course covered everything from basic HTML and CSS to more advanced topics like responsive design and JavaScript. Robert appreciated the course's structure, which allowed him to learn at his own pace and revisit lessons as needed. By the end of the course, he had built his own website and even started helping friends and family with their online projects. Robert's newfound skills boosted his confidence and opened up new opportunities for creative expression and community involvement.

Online learning offers a flexible, engaging, and accessible way for retirees to continue their educational journey. You can enrich your mind and stay intellectually active by choosing reputable platforms, exploring a wide range of subjects, and learning at your own pace. Whether you're interested in personal development, professional skills, or academic subjects, there's an online course out there that's perfect for you. So, why not take the plunge and discover the joys of lifelong learning?

Attending Local Workshops and Seminars

Imagine spending an afternoon learning to cook gourmet meals or mastering the basics of financial planning, all while meeting new people and sharing a few laughs. Local workshops and seminars offer hands-on learning in a supportive environment, making them an excellent option for retirees looking to stay engaged and socially active. These events provide practical skills that you can apply in your daily life, whether it's enhancing your culinary repertoire or understanding how to better manage your retirement funds. Additionally, the interactive format of workshops lets you practice new skills and ask questions in real-time, helping you thoroughly understand the subject matter.

Networking is another significant benefit of attending local workshops and seminars. These events are designed to bring together people with similar interests, providing a perfect setting for making new friends and professional connections. You'll find yourself in a room full of individuals who share your enthusiasm for learning, creating an instant camaraderie. Additionally, the insights gained from experts and practitioners can be invaluable. These professionals bring a wealth of knowledge and experience, offering practical tips and real-world advice that you can't get from books alone.

Finding and signing up for local workshops and seminars is generally quite easy. Start by checking community centers and libraries, which often host various educational events. These venues usually have bulletin boards or online calendars listing upcoming workshops. Event platforms like Eventbrite are also excellent resources for discovering local events tailored to your interests. Simply enter your location and the type of workshop you're interested in, and you'll find numerous options to choose from. Local universities and cultural institutions frequently offer public lectures and seminars as part of their outreach programs. These events are often open to the community and can cover various topics, from the arts to science and technology.

. . .

The types of workshops and seminars available are as diverse as your interests. If you have a flair for writing, consider enrolling in a creative writing workshop. These sessions provide a structured environment to hone your writing skills, whether you're working on a novel, memoir, or poetry. Financial planning seminars can be incredibly beneficial, especially if you want to optimize your retirement savings or understand investment options. These seminars often feature financial advisors who can answer your questions and guide you through complex financial landscapes. Cooking and culinary classes are another popular choice, offering the chance to learn new recipes and cooking techniques. Imagine the joy of preparing a delicious meal for your friends and family, knowing you've mastered the art of French cuisine or perfected your pasta-making skills.

Take the story of Emily, who improved her culinary skills through local classes. Emily had always enjoyed cooking but wanted to expand her repertoire beyond the basics. She found a series of culinary workshops at her community center, each focusing on a different type of cuisine. Over several months, Emily learned to prepare everything from Thai curries to Italian pastries. The hands-on nature of the classes allowed her to practice new techniques under the guidance of professional chefs. Emily gained confidence in the kitchen and made lasting friendships with her fellow culinary enthusiasts. Today, she regularly hosts themed dinner parties, impressing her guests with her newfound skills.

Then there's Mark, a retiree who learned to manage his finances better through a series of financial planning seminars. Mark had always been cautious with his money but felt overwhelmed by the complexities of retirement planning. He decided to attend a seminar series offered by a local financial institution. The seminars covered various topics, including investment strategies, estate planning, and tax optimization. Mark found the sessions incredibly informative, with financial advisors breaking down complex concepts into easy-to-understand terms. He left each seminar with actionable tips and a clearer understanding of how to manage his retirement savings effectively. Today, Mark feels more confident about his financial future and even shares his newfound knowledge with friends and family.

. . .

Local workshops and seminars offer an excellent way to learn and grow in retirement. They provide practical skills, social interaction, and valuable expert insights, making them an enriching and enjoyable experience. Whether you're interested in creative writing, financial planning, or cooking, a workshop can help you enhance your skills and meet like-minded individuals.

Learning a New Language

Imagine unlocking a world of new experiences simply by learning a few phrases in another language. This isn't just about communication; it's about enhancing your cognitive skills and deepening your understanding of different cultures. Studies show that learning a new language can improve memory and boost mental agility, which is especially beneficial as we age. It's like giving your brain a workout, keeping it sharp and engaged. Moreover, speaking another language can transform your travel experiences, allowing you to connect more meaningfully with locals and immerse yourself fully in the culture. Language opens doors to unique and enriching interactions, whether ordering a meal in Paris, haggling at a market in Mexico, or chatting with new friends in Tokyo.

Getting started with language learning can be exciting and daunting, but it becomes an enjoyable challenge with the right approach. Begin by choosing a language that interests you and is practical for your goals. You may have always been fascinated by French literature, or you may have family roots in Italy. The language you choose should resonate with you personally. Once you've made your choice, language learning apps like Duolingo and Babbel are excellent resources. These apps are user-friendly and offer structured lessons that you can complete at your own pace. They use gamification techniques to make learning fun, incorporating quizzes, flashcards, and interactive exercises that help reinforce your skills.

Joining language exchange groups can also enhance your learning experience. These groups pair you with native speakers who want to learn your language, creating a mutually beneficial exchange. You'll practice speaking and listening, gaining confidence and fluency. Language exchange groups can be found online or in your local community, providing opportunities to meet new people and share cultural insights. Additionally, consider attending language meetups or conversation clubs. These gatherings offer a relaxed environment to practice your skills and learn from others. They're often informal and welcoming, making them perfect for beginners and advanced learners.

Different methods and resources cater to various learning styles, so finding what works best for you is important. Online courses and tutorials provide structured learning and flexibility to study from home. Websites like Coursera and edX offer language courses from renowned institutions with video lectures, assignments, and peer interaction. If you prefer immersive experiences, language immersion programs can be incredibly effective. These programs place you in a setting where the target language is spoken exclusively, accelerating your learning through constant exposure and practice. For those who enjoy social learning, local language classes and meetups offer a classroom environment with face-to-face interaction. Many community centers and cultural institutions host these classes, providing expert instruction and a chance to practice with peers.

Consider the story of Maria, who became fluent in Spanish through a combination of apps and local classes. Maria had always wanted to learn Spanish to communicate better with her grandchildren, who were growing up bilingual. She started with Duolingo, dedicating a few minutes each day to practice. As her confidence grew, she enrolled in a local Spanish class, where she had the opportunity to converse with native speakers and receive personalized feedback. Over time, Maria's dedication paid off. She could hold conversations with her grandchildren, join in family gatherings, and she even traveled to Spain, where she navigated cities and towns with ease. Her new language skills enriched her family relationships and opened up a world of travel opportunities.

Then there's James, who used his newfound language skills during international travel. James had always dreamed of visiting Japan but felt intimidated by the language barrier. Determined to make the most of his trip, he began learning Japanese using Babbel and YouTube tutorials. He also joined a local language exchange group, where he practiced speaking with native Japanese speakers. By the time he embarked on his journey, James could greet locals, order food, and ask for directions in Japanese. His efforts were met with appreciation and warmth from the locals, making his travel experience deeply rewarding and immersive. James's story shows that learning a new language can transform your cognitive skills and life experiences, making every interaction richer and more meaningful.

Exploring History Through Local Museums

Imagine walking through the grand halls of a local museum; each exhibit is a gateway to another time and place. Museums offer a treasure trove of educational and cultural enrichment, allowing you to gain insights into both local and global history. They help you understand the events, people, and cultures that have shaped our world, providing context and deeper meaning to the present. Interactive and immersive exhibits make these experiences even more engaging. Whether it's a beautifully restored painting or a life-sized dinosaur skeleton, these displays capture your imagination and bring history to life. Supporting museums also means preserving cultural heritage for future generations, ensuring these stories and artifacts remain accessible and intact.

Finding and visiting local museums can be an enjoyable part of your retirement routine. Start by checking museum websites and local tourism guides. These resources often list current exhibits, special events, and visitor information. Many museums offer memberships and passes that provide benefits like free admission, guest passes, and discounts on special events. This can be a cost-effective way to explore multiple museums throughout the year. Participating in guided tours can add another layer of depth to your visits. Knowledgeable guides provide fascinating insights and answer any questions you may have, making your museum experience even more enriching.

There are many types of museums to explore, each catering to different interests. Art and cultural museums showcase the creative achievements of various civilizations, from ancient sculptures to contemporary paintings. They offer a window into the artistic expressions of different cultures and periods. Science and technology museums, on the other hand, focus on the wonders of the natural world and human innovation. These museums often feature hands-on exhibits that make learning about science and technology fun and interactive. Historical and heritage museums delve into the past, exploring significant events, people, and places that have shaped our world. These museums cover everything from local history to world-changing events, providing a comprehensive look at our collective heritage.

Meet Sarah, a retiree who regularly visited a local art museum. Sarah had always appreciated art but never had the time to delve deeply into it. After retiring, she purchased a membership to her city's art museum. She started visiting once a week, each time exploring a different exhibit. Over time, Sarah developed a keen eye for different art styles and periods. She began attending art lectures and workshops offered by the museum, further enriching her understanding and appreciation of art. Sarah found that these visits provided intellectual stimulation and a sense of peace and fulfillment. The museum became her sanctuary, a place where she could lose herself in the beauty and complexity of art.

. . .

Another inspiring example is Ken, a retiree who volunteered as a museum guide. Ken had always been passionate about history and wanted to share that passion with others. He approached a local historical museum and offered his services as a volunteer. After training, Ken started leading guided tours, sharing fascinating stories and insights about the exhibits. He found immense satisfaction in educating visitors and sparking their interest in history. Volunteering also allowed Ken to meet people who shared his passion, creating a new social circle that enriched his retirement. His role as a museum guide gave him a sense of purpose and connection, proving that museums offer valuable learning opportunities and community involvement opportunities.

Exploring history through local museums is a rewarding way to continue your educational journey in retirement. Museums provide a rich tapestry of knowledge and culture, engaging your mind and enriching your life. Whether admiring a masterpiece, learning about scientific breakthroughs, or delving into historical events, each visit offers a new adventure. Supporting these institutions ensures that they remain vibrant centers of learning and culture, benefiting both you and future generations. So, consider spending a day at a museum next time you want to do something meaningful. The insights and inspiration you gain will make every visit worthwhile.

Joining a Community College Class

Picture entering a classroom bustling with people from diverse backgrounds, all excited to learn something new. This is the vibrant atmosphere you'll find at community colleges. They offer an affordable and diverse range of learning opportunities that cater to various interests and goals. Whether you're looking to pick up a new hobby, gain professional skills, or simply engage in intellectual pursuits, community colleges have something for everyone. These institutions provide access to a wide range of subjects and courses, making it easy to find something that piques your interest. The diverse student body also enriches your learning experience as you engage with individuals from different backgrounds and ages. This diversity fosters a dynamic learning environment where ideas are exchanged freely, and everyone benefits from each other's experiences.

. . .

Community colleges are affordable and offer flexible options to suit your schedule. You can attend classes during the day, evening, or even on weekends, making it possible to fit learning into your retirement lifestyle. These institutions also provide numerous opportunities for personal and professional development. Whether you want to delve into creative arts, enhance your technological skills, or focus on health and wellness, community colleges have courses designed to help you achieve your goals. The supportive environment encourages lifelong learning and personal growth, making your educational experience both fulfilling and enjoyable.

Finding and enrolling in community college classes is straightforward, but a few practical tips can help you navigate it more smoothly. Start by exploring course catalogs and schedules available on the college's website. These catalogs provide detailed course information, including descriptions, prerequisites, and schedules. Understanding the enrollment process and requirements is essential. Most community colleges have an open admission policy, but you may need to complete a placement test or provide transcripts for specific courses. Consider both credit and non-credit courses. Credit courses can count toward a degree or certificate, while non-credit courses are often focused on personal enrichment and do not require exams or grading.

The variety of classes available at community colleges is extensive, catering to various interests. Consider enrolling in arts and crafts classes if you have a creative streak. These courses cover everything from painting and pottery to knitting and jewelry making, providing a hands-on experience that allows you to express your creativity. Technology and computer skills classes are another popular option. These courses can help you stay up-to-date with the latest software, learn how to use social media, or even dive into more advanced topics like coding and digital design. Health and wellness courses offer valuable insights into maintaining a healthy lifestyle. You can find classes on nutrition, yoga, meditation, and even fitness training, all designed to help you stay active and healthy.

Linda pursued a new hobby through a community college art class. She had always admired the beautiful paintings she saw in galleries but never thought she had the talent to create her own. After retiring, she decided to take a leap and enrolled in a beginner's painting class at her local community college. The supportive environment and expert instruction helped Linda develop her skills and gain confidence. Over time, she discovered a passion for painting and even started selling her artwork at local craft fairs. Linda's experience shows how a community college class can ignite a new passion and provide a sense of accomplishment.

Another inspiring example is Randall, a retiree who learned computer skills to stay connected with his family. Randall felt overwhelmed by technology and wanted to learn how to use email and social media to keep in touch with his grandchildren. He enrolled in a basic computer skills class at his community college. The instructor was patient and explained everything in simple terms, making it easy for Randall to follow along. By the end of the course, Randall could confidently send emails, share photos on social media, and even video chat with his grandchildren. This newfound skill helped Randall stay connected with his family and opened up a world of online resources and communities.

. . .

Community colleges offer a wealth of learning opportunities that can enrich your retirement. Whether you're looking to develop a new hobby, enhance your skills, or focus on personal growth, these institutions provide the necessary resources and support. The diverse range of courses, flexible schedules, and affordable tuition make community colleges an excellent choice for lifelong learning. Linda and Randall's experiences illustrate the transformative power of education and the joy of discovering new passions and skills in retirement.

Lifelong learning is a powerful tool that keeps your mind engaged, your skills sharp, and your life enriched. As we transition into the next chapter, we'll explore how you can give back to your community and find fulfillment through volunteering and social good.

7

VOLUNTEERING AND GIVING BACK

"As you grow older, you will discover that you have two hands - one for helping yourself, the other for helping others."

— AUDREY HEPBURN

Imagine waking up each day with a renewed sense of purpose, knowing that your actions positively impact the community. Volunteering in retirement offers a unique opportunity to give back, stay active, and build meaningful connections. It's a chance to use your skills and passions to help others while enriching your life. Volunteering can transform your retirement years into a period of growth, fulfillment, and joy.

Finding the Right Volunteer Opportunity

Aligning volunteer work with your interests and skills is crucial for maximizing impact and enjoyment. Volunteering in areas that resonate with your passions and strengths makes the experience more rewarding and meaningful. Start by assessing your strengths and passions. Reflect on what you enjoy doing and where your talents lie. Whether you have a knack for organizing events, a talent for teaching, or a passion for working with animals, there's a volunteer opportunity that can benefit from your expertise.

Identifying causes that resonate deeply with you is also essential. Think about the issues that matter most to you. Are you passionate about education, healthcare, environmental conservation, or social justice? Focusing on causes you care about ensures your volunteer work aligns with your values and interests. Consider your past professional experience and hobbies as well. Skills and knowledge gained from your career can be incredibly valuable in a volunteer setting. For example, if you have a background in marketing, consider helping a local charity with its outreach efforts. If you enjoy gardening, look for opportunities to volunteer at a community garden.

Finding the right volunteer opportunity requires some research and exploration. Volunteer matching websites like VolunteerMatch and Idealist are excellent resources for locating suitable positions. These websites allow you to search for opportunities based on location, interests, and availability. You can find roles ranging from administrative support to direct service positions, ensuring there's something for everyone. Contacting local non-profits and community centers is another effective way to discover volunteer opportunities. Many organizations welcome volunteers and can provide information on how to get involved. Joining volunteer fairs and networking events can also help you connect with organizations and learn about available roles.

There are various volunteer roles to consider, each catering to different interests and skills. Administrative support for non-profits is a valuable contribution that helps organizations run smoothly.

Tasks may include answering phones, managing databases, or assisting with fundraising. Event planning and coordination roles may be perfect if you enjoy planning and organizing. These positions involve organizing events, managing logistics, and coordinating volunteers. Direct service roles, such as working with clients or animals, offer hands-on opportunities to make a difference. Whether helping at a food bank, mentoring youth, or caring for animals at a shelter, these roles provide direct interaction and immediate impact.

Consider the story of Nancy, a retiree who used her marketing skills to help a local charity. Nancy had a successful career in marketing and wanted to use her expertise to give back. She connected with a charity that needed help with its social media and outreach efforts. Nancy developed a comprehensive marketing plan, created engaging content, and managed their social media accounts. Her efforts significantly increased the charity's visibility and donations. Nancy found immense satisfaction in knowing that her skills were helping a cause she cared about, and the charity benefited greatly from her expertise.

. . .

Another inspiring example is William, who volunteered at a community garden. William had always enjoyed gardening but never had the time to fully pursue it during his working years. In retirement, he decided to volunteer at a local community garden. He spent his days planting, weeding, and harvesting crops. William also shared his gardening knowledge with other volunteers and community members. The garden flourished under his care, providing fresh produce for local families in need. William found joy in working with the earth and connecting with others who shared his passion for gardening.

Volunteering in retirement is a powerful way to give back, stay active, and build meaningful connections. By aligning volunteer work with your interests and skills, you can maximize the impact and enjoyment of the experience. Assess your strengths and passions, identify causes that resonate deeply, and consider your past professional experience and hobbies. Use volunteer matching websites, contact local non-profits, and join volunteer fairs to find suitable opportunities. Explore different volunteer roles, from administrative support and event planning to direct service positions. Let the stories of Nancy and William inspire you to find a volunteer opportunity that brings you fulfillment and joy.

Mentoring and Tutoring Programs

Imagine the satisfaction of helping a young person grasp the complexities of algebra or guiding them through the maze of career choices. Mentoring and tutoring provide a unique opportunity to significantly impact individuals and communities. These roles offer more than just academic or professional support; they provide guidance and encouragement, fostering growth and confidence in the recipients. By sharing your knowledge and expertise, you help shape the future of younger generations. This exchange builds meaningful, intergenerational relationships that enrich both your life and theirs, creating a lasting bond based on mutual respect and learning.

Getting started with mentoring and tutoring begins with identifying your areas of expertise and interest. Reflect on your professional background and personal passions. You may excel in math, have a knack for writing, or possess valuable career insights. These strengths can be the foundation of your mentoring or tutoring endeavors.

Once you've pinpointed your skills, contact schools, colleges, and youth organizations. These institutions often have programs and seek experienced individuals to join their efforts. Be prepared to undergo necessary background checks and training, as safeguarding the well-being of young people is a top priority in these roles.

There are various mentoring and tutoring programs to consider, each catering to different skills and interests. Academic tutoring for students is a popular and impactful option. Whether it's helping with homework, preparing for exams, or explaining complex concepts, your support can make a significant difference in a student's academic journey. Career mentoring for young professionals is another valuable avenue. By sharing your career experiences and offering advice, you can guide young adults through the challenges of entering the workforce and advancing in their careers. Life skills coaching for at-risk youth is equally important. These programs teach essential life skills, such as financial literacy, time management, and effective communication, providing young people with the tools they need to succeed.

. . .

Consider the story of David, a retired engineer who decided to help students improve their math skills. David had always enjoyed math and wanted to share his passion with others. He contacted a local high school and began tutoring students struggling with algebra and geometry. Through his patience and clear explanations, David helped many students gain confidence and improve their grades. The joy of seeing his students succeed and the gratitude he received from them made his retirement years incredibly fulfilling.

Another inspiring example is Diane, who guided a young professional through career challenges. After retiring from a successful career in marketing, Diane wanted to give back by mentoring young professionals in her field. She connected with a local college's career center and was paired with Sarah, a recent graduate struggling to find her footing in the marketing world. Diane gave Sarah valuable advice on job searching, networking, and personal brand development. Over time, Sarah secured a job at a reputable marketing firm and continued to seek Diane's guidance as she advanced in her career. The bond they formed went beyond professional advice, evolving into a meaningful friendship.

. . .

Mentoring and tutoring are not just about imparting knowledge but about fostering growth, building confidence, and creating lasting relationships. These roles offer a unique opportunity to help individuals and communities. You can enrich your retirement years and leave a lasting legacy by providing guidance and support to younger generations, sharing your knowledge and expertise, and building meaningful intergenerational relationships. Reflect on your expertise and interest, reach out to schools, colleges, and youth organizations, and explore the various mentoring and tutoring programs available. Whether it's academic tutoring, career mentoring, or life skills coaching, your contribution can make a world of difference. Let the stories of David and Diane inspire you to become a mentor or tutor, bringing fulfillment and purpose to your retirement.

Environmental Conservation Projects

Imagine standing in a lush forest, planting a tree that will grow tall and strong, providing a home for wildlife and a source of clean air for generations to come. Environmental conservation is not just about protecting nature; it's about preserving the planet for future generations and enhancing the well-being of communities. Volunteering in this area allows you to make a tangible impact on the environment while promoting sustainability and eco-friendly practices. By protecting natural habitats and wildlife, you help maintain biodiversity and ensure that ecosystems remain balanced and healthy. Promoting sustainability through conservation efforts encourages eco-friendly practices that benefit both the planet and its people. Enhancing community green spaces, such as parks and gardens, creates beautiful, healthy environments for everyone to enjoy.

Finding and participating in conservation projects starts with reaching out to local environmental organizations. These groups often have ongoing projects and always need dedicated volunteers. Contacting them directly can provide information on how to get involved and what roles are available. Participating in community clean-up events is another excellent way to contribute. Often organized by local governments or non-profits, these events focus on cleaning up parks, rivers, and beaches. They provide a hands-on way to make a difference and often turn into community gatherings where you can meet like-minded individuals.

Joining conservation groups and initiatives offers further opportunities for involvement. These groups work on various projects, from tree planting to wildlife monitoring, and provide a structured way to participate in conservation efforts.

Environmental conservation projects come in many forms, catering to different interests and skills. Tree planting and reforestation projects are fundamental to restoring natural habitats and combating climate change. These projects involve planting native trees in deforested areas, ensuring that they thrive and contribute to the ecosystem. Beach and river clean-ups focus on removing litter and pollutants from waterways, protecting marine life, and maintaining clean, beautiful beaches. Wildlife monitoring and habitat restoration projects involve tracking animal populations, restoring natural habitats, and ensuring that wildlife has a safe and healthy environment in which to live.

Consider the story of Jack, a retiree who volunteered with a local reforestation project. Jack had always loved the outdoors and wanted to impact the environment in a positive way. He joined a local group dedicated to reforesting a nearby park that had lost many trees due to disease. Jack spent his weekends planting young trees, caring for them, and educating visitors about the importance of reforestation. Over time, he saw the park transform into a vibrant, green space full of wildlife. Jack felt a deep sense of accomplishment, knowing that his efforts were helping to restore the natural beauty of the area and provide a habitat for countless species.

Another inspiring example is Carol, who helped organize community clean-up events. Carol had a background in event planning and wanted to use her skills to benefit the environment. She teamed up with a local environmental organization to plan monthly clean-up events at various parks and rivers in her city. Carol coordinated volunteers, arranged for supplies, and promoted the events through social media and local news outlets. The clean-up events attracted diverse participants, from families to college students, all eager to make a difference. Carol's organizational skills ensured that each event ran smoothly and effectively, resulting in cleaner, healthier green spaces for the community.

. . .

Environmental conservation projects offer a rewarding way to give back to the planet and your community. Protecting natural habitats, promoting sustainability, and enhancing green spaces contribute to a healthier, more beautiful world. Finding the right project involves contacting local environmental organizations, participating in community clean-up events, and joining conservation groups. Whether you're planting trees, cleaning up beaches, or monitoring wildlife, your efforts make a significant impact. Let the stories of Jack and Carol inspire you to get involved and make a positive difference in the environment.

Participating in Local Charity Events

Imagine the energy of a bustling town square filled with neighbors, friends, and even strangers coming together for a local charity event. These events offer a sense of purpose and community, turning ordinary days into extraordinary ones. Charity events provide immediate and tangible support to communities by raising funds and awareness for important causes. They bring people together, fostering a sense of unity and collective effort, which builds community spirit and engagement. Whether it's through fundraising walks, charity auctions, or food drives, these events offer direct assistance to those in need, making a visible impact on many lives.

Finding and participating in charity events can be straightforward yet deeply rewarding. Start by checking local event listings and community bulletins, often found in libraries, community centers, or local newspapers. These sources frequently advertise upcoming events and provide details on how you can get involved. Contacting charities and non-profits is another excellent way to discover opportunities. Many organizations are eager for volunteers and can provide information on ongoing or upcoming events. Volunteering for event planning and coordination allows you to play a crucial role behind the scenes, ensuring everything runs smoothly and effectively. This role can be deeply satisfying as you see the event come together and witness the positive impact it creates.

Charity events come in various forms, catering to different interests and skills. Fundraising walks and runs are popular options that combine physical activity with philanthropy. Participants often gather sponsors who pledge donations based on the distance walked or run. These events raise substantial funds and promote health and fitness within the community. Charity auctions and galas offer a more formal way to support causes. These events often involve bidding on donated items or experiences, with all proceeds going to the chosen charity. They provide an opportunity for socializing, networking, and enjoying an elegant evening while contributing to a good cause. Food drives and distribution events focus on collecting and distributing food to those in need. Volunteers can sort and pack food, distribute it to families, or organize food collection points around the community.

Consider the story of Shirley, who regularly volunteers at local food drives. After retiring, Shirley wanted to stay active and give back to her community. She started volunteering with a local food bank that organizes monthly food drives. Shirley's role involves sorting donations, packing food boxes, and distributing them to families in need. Each time, she sees the gratitude on the faces of those she helps, which fills her with a profound sense of purpose and fulfillment. Shirley's consistent efforts have made her a valued member of the food bank team, and she has also formed deep connections with fellow volunteers.

Another inspiring example is Steven, a retiree who helped organize a successful charity auction. With a background in event planning, Steven decided to use his skills for a good cause. He teamed up with a local non-profit to plan an annual charity auction. Steven's responsibilities included securing auction items, coordinating with vendors, and promoting the event. His meticulous planning and dedication ensured the auction was a resounding success, raising significant funds for the charity. The event provided much-needed financial support and brought the community together for an enjoyable and meaningful evening. Steven found immense satisfaction in seeing his efforts translate into real-world benefits for those in need.

Participating in local charity events offers a unique way to give back to your community. These events provide immediate and tangible support, raising funds and awareness for important causes while building community spirit and engagement. By checking local event listings, contacting charities, and volunteering for event planning, you can find numerous opportunities to get involved. From fundraising walks and charity auctions to food drives, various types of charity events suit different interests and skills. Let the stories of Shirley and Steven inspire you to participate in local charity events, bringing fulfillment and joy to your retirement.

Voluntourism: Combining Travel and Volunteering

Imagine exploring a new country while making meaningful contributions to its communities. Voluntourism offers a unique blend of travel and community service, allowing you to experience new cultures while giving back. This type of travel isn't just about sightseeing; it's about building connections with local communities and gaining a sense of fulfillment and purpose. By engaging in voluntourism, you immerse yourself in the local way of life, understand its challenges, and contribute to solutions that make a real difference.

Finding reputable voluntourism programs requires careful research. Start by exploring websites and organizations specializing in volunteer travel, such as Volunteer HQ and Projects Abroad.

These organizations offer a range of opportunities across different countries and causes. Reading reviews and testimonials from past volunteers can provide valuable insights into the quality and impact of the programs. Look for feedback on the organization's support, the living conditions, and the overall experience. It's also important to consider the alignment of your skills and interests with the program's needs. Choose a project where your abilities can make the most impact, whether it's teaching, conservation, or community development.

Voluntourism projects come in many forms, catering to various interests and skills. Teaching English in rural schools is a popular option. Many communities lack access to quality education, and your expertise can help bridge that gap. You'll work with local teachers, develop lesson plans, and engage with students, enhancing their language skills and opening up new opportunities for them. Wildlife conservation projects are another exciting avenue. These projects often involve working in nature reserves or wildlife sanctuaries, helping with research, animal care, and habitat restoration. It's a chance to contribute to preserving endangered species and learn about conservation efforts firsthand. Community development initiatives focus on improving the living conditions and infrastructure in underprivileged areas. You could assist in building schools, installing clean water systems, or supporting local healthcare initiatives. These projects provide tangible benefits to communities, making a lasting impact on their quality of life.

Consider the story of Rachel, who taught English in a remote village in Thailand. Rachel had always dreamed of visiting Southeast Asia and wanted to do more than just travel. She found a voluntourism program through Volunteer HQ and spent three months teaching English to children in a small village. The experience was transformative. Rachel helped the students improve their language skills and formed deep bonds with the community. She participated in local festivals, learned about Thai culture, and even picked up some of the language. Rachel's presence in the village left a lasting impact, and she returned home with a profound sense of fulfillment and a broader perspective on life.

. . .

Then there's Mike and Judith, a retired couple who participated in an African wildlife conservation project. They had always been passionate about animals and wanted to contribute to their preservation. Through Projects Abroad, they joined a program in Kenya focused on protecting elephants and rhinos. Their days included tracking animals, collecting data, and assisting with anti-poaching efforts. The couple also engaged with local communities, educating them about the importance of wildlife conservation. Mike and Judith's efforts helped protect these majestic creatures and fostered a connection with the local people. They returned home with unforgettable memories and a deeper appreciation for the natural world.

Voluntourism allows you to combine the thrill of travel with the satisfaction of making a positive impact. By researching reputable programs, considering your skills and interests, and choosing a project that resonates with you, you can create an enriching and meaningful experience. Whether you teach English in rural schools, participate in wildlife conservation, or assist in community development, the benefits are immense. You'll experience new cultures, build connections, and gain a sense of fulfillment and purpose that traditional travel can't match. Let the stories of Rachel, Mike, and Judith inspire you to explore voluntourism and make your retirement a time of adventure and giving back.

Volunteering and giving back can transform your retirement into a period of growth, fulfillment, and joy. From local charity events to global voluntourism, the opportunities are endless. In the next chapter, we'll explore how you can achieve financial peace of mind, ensuring you can enjoy these enriching experiences without financial worry.

8

FINANCIAL PEACE OF MIND

"As in all successful ventures, the foundation of a good retirement is planning."

— EARL NIGHTINGALE

You're sitting at your kitchen table, sipping a cup of coffee as you review your monthly expenses on a budgeting app. The feeling of control and confidence that comes from knowing exactly where your money is going can be incredibly empowering. In retirement, managing your finances becomes more important than ever. A well-thought-out budget can help you live comfortably and securely without financial uncertainty.

Crafting a retirement budget isn't just about cutting costs; it's about making informed decisions that align with your new lifestyle.

Budgeting for Your New Lifestyle

Creating a retirement budget is essential for managing expenses and ensuring financial stability. It starts with assessing your current and future expenses. Think about your monthly bills—housing, utilities, groceries, and transportation. Then, consider variable expenses, such as dining out, entertainment, and travel. Don't forget to account for occasional costs like home repairs or medical expenses. By understanding your expenses, you can create a realistic budget that covers all aspects of your life.

Identifying sources of income is the next step. Retirement often means a shift from a regular paycheck to other income streams. These include Social Security benefits, pensions, retirement savings accounts, and any part-time work or freelance opportunities that you may participate in. Knowing exactly how much money you have coming in each month allows you to plan accordingly and avoid overspending.

. . .

Tracking your spending habits is another vital component. This helps you see where your money is going and identify areas where you could cut back. Budgeting apps and software can be invaluable tools in this process. Apps like Mint and YNAB (You Need A Budget) allow you to categorize expenses, set spending limits, and track progress. Simplifi by Quicken is another excellent option, simplifying budgeting to under five minutes a week by automatically categorizing your spending and setting spending limits. These tools offer a clear picture of your financial health and help you stay on track.

When setting up your budget, start by categorizing your expenses into essential categories like housing, healthcare, and leisure. Housing may include your mortgage or rent, utilities, and maintenance costs. Healthcare can cover insurance premiums, medications, and routine check-ups. Leisure expenses encompass dining out, hobbies, and travel. Setting realistic spending limits for each category ensures you stay within your means while enjoying your retirement.

. . .

Avoiding common financial pitfalls is critical to maintaining a healthy budget. Overspending on discretionary items like dining out or shopping can quickly consume your savings. It's easy to underestimate healthcare costs, which can be significant as you age. Be sure to factor in potential medical expenses, including long-term care, if needed. Ignoring inflation and rising living costs can also be a mistake. Prices for everyday items can increase over time, so it's important to adjust your budget periodically to reflect these changes.

Consider the story of Bill, a retiree who used a budgeting app to track and reduce his expenses. Bill found that he was spending more on dining out than he realized. Using Mint, he categorized his costs and set a monthly dining-out limit. This simple change saved him hundreds of dollars each month, which he redirected toward his travel fund. Bill's experience shows how powerful budgeting tools can be in helping you manage your finances effectively.

Another inspiring example is Elizabeth, who adjusted her lifestyle to fit her budget. Elizabeth realized that her housing costs consumed a large portion of her income. She downsized to a smaller home, significantly reducing her expenses. The money she saved allowed her to enjoy other activities, like gardening and taking classes at the local community center. Elizabeth's story illustrates the impact of thoughtful budgeting and lifestyle adjustments on your financial well-being.

Creating a retirement budget may seem daunting, but it's crucial to ensure financial peace of mind. You can create a budget that supports your new lifestyle by assessing your expenses, identifying income sources, and tracking your spending. Using budgeting apps and setting realistic spending limits can help you stay on track and avoid common financial pitfalls. The success stories of Bill and Elizabeth demonstrate the positive outcomes that careful budgeting can achieve. So, take control of your finances and enjoy the confidence of knowing your retirement is secure.

Exploring Part-Time Work and Freelance Opportunities

Retirement doesn't mean you have to stop working entirely. Many retirees find that part-time work or freelancing offers a perfect balance of staying active and supplementing their income. Imagine waking up each day with a sense of purpose, knowing that you're doing something you love and getting paid for it. These opportunities provide financial benefits and keep you engaged, helping to stave off boredom and loneliness. Whether you're looking to pursue a long-held passion or simply want to stay busy, part-time work can bring both fulfillment and financial rewards.

One of the primary benefits of part-time work and freelancing is the ability to supplement your retirement income. While Social Security and pensions provide a safety net, additional income from part-time work can give you more financial freedom. It allows you to cover unexpected expenses, indulge in travel, or pursue hobbies without worrying about stretching your budget. Moreover, staying active through work can have significant mental and emotional benefits. Engaging in meaningful activities keeps your mind sharp and provides a sense of accomplishment. Whether it's using your skills in a new way or learning something entirely different, part-time work can be both stimulating and rewarding.

. . .

Finding part-time work or freelance opportunities may seem challenging, but there are numerous resources to help you. Job search websites like Indeed and FlexJobs offer various part-time positions tailored to various skills and interests. These platforms allow you to filter your search based on location, industry, and work schedule, making it easier to find the perfect fit. Networking with former colleagues and industry contacts can also open new opportunities. Don't hesitate to reach out and let people know you're looking for part-time work; personal connections often lead to the best opportunities. Exploring platforms like Upwork and Fiverr can also be fruitful. These sites connect freelancers with clients seeking specific skills, such as writing, graphic design, or administrative support. They offer the flexibility to work on projects that interest you and set your own schedule.

There are numerous part-time and freelance roles to consider, catering to various skills and interests. Consulting and advisory roles are ideal for those with extensive experience in a particular field. These positions allow you to share your expertise and provide valuable guidance to businesses or individuals. Creative freelancing, such as writing, graphic design, or photography, offers an outlet for artistic expression while earning income. Part-time retail or customer service positions can be a great fit if you enjoy interacting with people. These roles often offer flexible schedules and the opportunity to stay socially engaged.

Consider the story of Gloria, a retiree who turned her hobby into a successful freelance career. Gloria had always loved crafting handmade jewelry, and after retiring, she decided to sell her creations online. She started small, opening an Etsy shop and promoting her products on social media. Her unique designs quickly gained popularity, and soon, Gloria received orders from all over the country. The additional income allowed her to invest in better materials and expand her business. Gloria's passion for jewelry-making provided financial benefits and immense personal satisfaction.

Another inspiring example is Tony, who found fulfillment in a part-time teaching role. After retiring from a long career in engineering, Tony realized he missed the interaction and intellectual challenge his job provided. He applied for a part-time position at a local community college, teaching introductory engineering courses. The role allowed him to share his knowledge and experience with the next generation of engineers while maintaining a flexible schedule. Tony found great joy in mentoring his students and watching them succeed. His part-time teaching job renewed his purpose and connected him with a vibrant academic community.

Exploring part-time work and freelance opportunities can significantly enhance your retirement experience. It offers a way to stay financially secure, keep your mind active, and pursue passions that bring you joy. Whether it's turning a hobby into a business, consulting in your field of expertise, or teaching others, the possibilities are endless. Embrace the opportunities that come your way, and find fulfillment in this new chapter of your life.

Maximizing Social Security Benefits

Understanding Social Security benefits is crucial for anyone planning their retirement. These benefits can significantly impact your financial well-being, making it essential to know how they work and how to maximize them. Determining your eligibility and benefit amounts is the first step. Your Social Security benefits are calculated based on your thirty-five highest-earning years. If you have fewer than thirty-five years of earnings, zeros are averaged in, which can lower your benefit amount. Therefore, working for at least thirty-five years can help maximize your benefits.

The age at which you claim your benefits also plays a significant role in how much you will receive. The earliest you can start receiving Social Security is age sixty-two, but doing so will reduce your benefits. Waiting until your full retirement age (FRA), which is between sixty-six and sixty-seven, depending on your birth year, allows you to receive full benefits. Delaying benefits even further, up to age seventy, can increase your monthly payments by approximately 8 percent annually. This can make a substantial difference in your retirement income.

Spousal and survivor benefits are additional aspects to consider. If you are married, you may be eligible to receive benefits based on your spouse's earnings record, up to 50 percent of their benefit amount. This can be particularly advantageous if your earnings are lower than your spouse's. In the event of your spouse's death, you may be eligible for survivor benefits, which can be up to 100 percent of your spouse's benefit amount. Understanding these options can help you make informed decisions that maximize your benefits.

One effective strategy to maximize your Social Security benefits is to delay claiming them. For example, if you can wait until age seventy, your benefits will be significantly higher than if you start at age sixty-two. This approach is particularly beneficial if you expect to live a long life, as the higher monthly payments will accumulate over time. Coordinating benefits with your spouse can also be advantageous. For instance, one spouse could claim benefits early while the other delays, balancing immediate needs with long-term gains.

If you continue to work while receiving Social Security benefits, it's crucial to understand how this affects your payments. Earnings above a certain threshold can reduce your benefits if you are below your FRA. However, once you reach your FRA, there is no penalty for continuing to work, and your benefits may even increase if you have additional high-earning years. Evaluating the impact of continued employment on your benefits can help you make the best decision for your financial situation.

Misconceptions and mistakes related to Social Security benefits are common, and avoiding them can save you from financial pitfalls. One common misconception is that Social Security benefits are fixed and unchangeable. Your benefits can increase if you continue working and earning more. Another mistake is overlooking the impact of early retirement on your benefits. Claiming benefits before your FRA can reduce your monthly payments by up to 30 percent, adding to significant losses over time. Ignoring the tax implications of Social Security income is another error to avoid. Depending on your total income, up to 85 percent of your Social Security benefits could be taxable. Understanding these issues can help you avoid costly mistakes.

Consider the story of Robert, who decided to delay his Social Security benefits until age seventy. By waiting, he increased his monthly payments significantly. This decision provided him with a higher, more stable income throughout his retirement. Robert's experience highlights the benefits of delaying Social Security to maximize your monthly payments.

Another example is Clara and Marty, who coordinated their Social Security benefits for maximum efficiency. Marty claimed his benefits at his FRA to provide immediate income, while Clara delayed hers until age seventy. This strategy allowed them to balance their short-term and long-term financial needs effectively. Their careful planning ensured a higher combined income, providing financial security throughout their retirement.

Understanding and maximizing your Social Security benefits can significantly improve your retirement income. By determining eligibility, considering the impact of claiming age, and exploring spousal and survivor benefits, you can make informed decisions that enhance your financial well-being. Delaying benefits, coordinating with a spouse, and evaluating the impact of continued employment are practical strategies to consider.

Avoiding common misconceptions and mistakes will help you make the most of your benefits, ensuring a more secure and comfortable retirement.

Downsizing and Simplifying Your Home

Stepping into a home that feels open, light, and easy to navigate can be a great feeling. Downsizing and simplifying your living space can bring a sense of freedom and reduce daily stress. One of the significant benefits of downsizing is lower housing and maintenance costs. A smaller home means fewer rooms to heat, cool, clean, and repair. This can lead to substantial savings on utilities and upkeep, allowing you to allocate your funds to other areas of your life, like travel or hobbies.

Reducing clutter is another advantage of downsizing. Over the years, it's easy to accumulate items that we no longer need or use. Simplifying your home by decluttering can create more living space and make your environment more enjoyable. It also makes it easier to find things, leading to a more organized and peaceful life. Enhancing mobility and accessibility is particularly important as we age. Moving to a smaller, single-story home or an apartment can eliminate the need for stairs, making it easier to get around and reducing the risk of falls. This is especially beneficial if you have mobility issues or anticipate needing a more accessible living space in the future.

The downsizing process begins with assessing your current housing needs and options. Consider what is most important to you in a home. Do you need a large yard, or would a smaller patio suffice? Is it essential to be close to family and friends, or are you looking for a quiet retreat? Once you understand your needs clearly, explore different housing options. Moving to a smaller home or apartment can significantly reduce your living expenses and simplify your life. Retirement communities or senior living facilities offer additional benefits, such as on-site amenities, social activities, and medical support. Co-housing or shared living arrangements are also worth considering if you enjoy a communal lifestyle and want to share expenses and responsibilities.

Decluttering and organizing your belongings is an essential step in the downsizing process. Start by sorting through each room and deciding what to keep, donate, sell, or discard. Be honest about what you truly need and use. Items with sentimental value can be the hardest to part with, but remember that memories are not tied to physical objects. Take photos of cherished items before letting them go, or consider passing them on to family members who might appreciate them. Selling or donating unnecessary items can also provide a sense of satisfaction. Many charities and organizations are grateful for gently used furniture, clothing, and household goods. You can also use online platforms like Craigslist or Facebook Marketplace to sell items and make some extra cash.

Consider the story of Gary and Susan, who moved to a smaller home after retiring. Their large family home had become too much to maintain, and they wanted to free up some finances for travel. They sold their house and purchased a cozy two-bedroom cottage. The move significantly reduced their expenses, and the smaller space was easier to manage. They now have more time and money to enjoy their hobbies and spend time with their grandchildren. Downsizing allowed them to simplify their lives and focus on what truly matters.

. . .

Another inspiring example is Martha, who found a supportive community in a senior living facility. After her husband passed away, Martha felt isolated in her suburban home. She decided to move to a senior living community where she could be closer to people her age. The facility offered various social activities, fitness classes, and on-site healthcare services. Martha quickly made new friends and found a renewed sense of purpose. The move simplified her life and enriched it in ways she hadn't anticipated.

Downsizing and simplifying your home can bring numerous benefits, from reducing expenses to enhancing your living environment. You can create a more manageable and enjoyable living situation by assessing your needs, decluttering your space, and exploring different housing options. The stories of Gary, Susan, and Martha illustrate the positive impact of downsizing on your life.

Smart Investing for Retirees

Imagine sitting with your morning coffee, reviewing your investment portfolio, and feeling a sense of security and growth. Smart investing in retirement is not just about preserving what you have; it's about making your money work for you, providing financial security and potential growth. Strategic investments can ensure you have enough funds to enjoy your golden years without worrying about running out of money. Diversifying your investment portfolio is critical to balancing risk and return. By spreading your investments across various asset classes like stocks, bonds, and real estate, you minimize the impact of any single investment's poor performance. This approach helps protect your nest egg and provides a smoother ride in the often volatile markets.

Balancing risk and return is essential for retirees. Finding the right mix of investments that offer growth potential without exposing you to undue risk is crucial. As you age, you may want to shift more toward lower-risk investments. However, keeping a portion in growth-oriented assets can help combat inflation and ensure your money retains its purchasing power. Generating passive income through investments is another important strategy. Investing in dividend stocks or bonds can provide a steady income stream, supplementing your retirement savings and covering daily expenses.

. . .

Allocating assets based on risk tolerance and time horizon is the foundation of a sound investment strategy. If you're more risk-averse, you may prefer a higher allocation in bonds and dividend-paying stocks. If you have a longer time horizon or a higher tolerance for risk, you might include more growth-oriented stocks. Low-cost index funds and ETFs are excellent choices for retirees. These funds offer broad market exposure, reducing risk through diversification while keeping costs low. The lower fees mean more of your money stays invested, working for you. Income-generating investments like dividend stocks and bonds can provide reliable income. Dividend stocks pay regular dividends, often quarterly, while bonds pay interest, usually semi-annually. Both can be valuable additions to a retiree's portfolio, offering income without selling assets.

Avoiding common investment mistakes is crucial for maintaining financial health in retirement. Expecting high returns without considering the associated risks can be disastrous. Investments promising unusually high returns often come with high risk, which may not be suitable for retirees. Ignoring fees and expenses can eat away at your returns. Even small fees can compound over time, significantly reducing your overall gains. Regularly rebalancing your portfolio is another essential practice. As the market fluctuates, your asset allocation can drift from its target. Rebalancing ensures your portfolio remains aligned with your risk tolerance and investment goals.

Consider the story of Alice, who built a diversified portfolio for steady income. Alice worked with a financial advisor to create a mix of stocks, bonds, and real estate investments. She included dividend-paying stocks and municipal bonds, which provided regular income. Her diversified approach protected her from market volatility, ensuring a steady income stream and financial peace of mind. Alice's experience highlights the importance of a well-balanced, diversified portfolio.

Another inspiring example is Joe, who avoided common investment mistakes and achieved financial security. Joe initially invested in high-return, high-risk stocks, hoping for quick gains. After experiencing significant losses, he learned the importance of balancing risk and return. He shifted his focus to low-cost index funds and income-generating investments. Joe also became diligent about monitoring fees and regularly rebalancing his portfolio. This disciplined approach helped him recover from his losses and build a secure financial future.

Smart investing in retirement is about making informed decisions that align with your financial goals and risk tolerance. Diversifying your portfolio, balancing risk and return, and generating passive income are essential strategies. Avoiding common mistakes like chasing high returns and ignoring fees can protect your investments and ensure long-term financial health. The stories of Alice and Joe illustrate the positive outcomes of strategic investing. Embrace these principles, and enjoy the financial peace of mind that comes with a well-managed investment portfolio.

In summary, Chapter 8 has provided valuable insights into managing your finances in retirement, from budgeting to investing. These strategies can help ensure financial stability and security. As we move forward, let's explore how understanding technological advances and developing digital skills can enrich your retirement experience.

9

TECHNOLOGY AND DIGITAL SKILLS

"Technology is best when it brings people together."

— MATT MULLENWEG

Reconnecting with a high school buddy you haven't seen in decades can reignite a connection with a past friendship. Understanding technology and enhancing your digital skills can make this happen! This is the magic of social media—a powerful tool that can bridge miles and years, bringing people together in once unimaginable ways. For retirees, mastering social media platforms offers numerous benefits, from enhancing social connections to staying informed about the latest news and events. Whether catching up with family, joining interest-based groups, or simply staying in the loop, social media can enrich your life in countless ways.

Mastering Social Media Platforms

Social media can be a lifeline for retirees. It provides an easy and convenient way to reconnect with old friends and family members who may be scattered across the globe. Imagine the joy of rediscovering a long-lost cousin or catching up with a former colleague. Social media platforms like Facebook offer a space where you can share photos, send messages, and even video chat, making it feel like those miles melt away. It's not just about reconnecting with people you already know; social media also allows you to join groups and communities based on your interests. Whether you're passionate about gardening, travel, or classic movies, there's a group for you. These communities can provide support, share tips, and even become a source of new friendships.

To set up Facebook, refer to Chapter 2: Using Technology to Stay Connected. This will help you get connected. Once you are set up on Facebook, you can join groups based on your interests. Type a keyword like "gardening" into the search bar, find a group that appeals to you, and click "Join."

Instagram is another platform that can enhance your social connections. Unlike Facebook, which is more text-focused, Instagram is all about sharing photos and videos. Download the Instagram app from your smartphone's app store to get started (there is no functional version for computers). Open the app and sign up using your email or phone number. Once your account is created, you can follow friends, family, and even celebrities or public figures. To share your photos, tap the "+" icon, choose a picture from your gallery or take a new one, and add a caption. Hashtags are a great way to connect with others interested in the same topics. For example, if you love bird-watching, use hashtags like #birdwatching or #naturephotography. Instagram also offers Stories, which are temporary posts that disappear after twenty-four hours, perfect for sharing quick updates or daily highlights.

LinkedIn is another valuable platform, especially if you're interested in professional networking or exploring new career opportunities. Start by creating an account on the LinkedIn website. Fill out your profile with details about your career, education, and skills. Upload a professional-looking photo and write a summary highlighting your experience and interests. LinkedIn allows you to connect with former colleagues, join professional groups, and follow companies or thought leaders in your industry. It's a fantastic way to stay connected professionally, even in retirement. You can also share articles, comment on posts, and participate in group discussions, keeping your professional skills sharp.

While social media offers numerous benefits, it's essential to use it safely. Start by adjusting your privacy settings on each platform. On Facebook, for instance, you can control who sees your posts by clicking "Settings" and then "Privacy." You can make your posts visible to friends only, limiting the audience. Managing your followers is also crucial. If someone is bothering you or you don't want them to see your content, you can block them. Avoid sharing sensitive information online, such as your home address, phone number, or financial details. Scams and phishing attempts are common, so be cautious about accepting friend requests from strangers or clicking on suspicious links.

Consider the story of Nancy, a retiree who reconnected with her high school friends through Facebook. They started a private group where they shared photos, reminisced about old times, and even planned reunions. This group has become a significant source of joy and connection for Nancy.

Another example is Bill, who joined an Instagram group for vintage car enthusiasts. Through this group, he learned a lot about car restoration and made new friends who shared his passion. These stories highlight social media's positive impact on life, making it a tool worth mastering.

Creating and Maintaining a Blog

Blogging offers retirees an excellent way to express thoughts and share experiences creatively. Imagine writing about your travels, hobbies, or life lessons and having an audience eager to read and engage with your content. Blogging can serve as an outlet to document adventures, whether a road trip across the country, favorite recipes you have collected over the years or a new gardening project in your backyard. It's a platform to connect with readers and build a community around shared interests. Writing and sharing can be deeply fulfilling, providing a sense of purpose and accomplishment.

Setting up a blog is simpler than you may think. Start by choosing a blogging platform that suits your needs. WordPress and Blogger are both popular options. WordPress offers flexibility with a wide range of plugins and themes, while Blogger is user-friendly and integrates well with Google services. Once you've chosen your platform, you'll need to select a domain name. Think of something catchy and relevant to your blog's theme. For example, if you're blogging about gardening, a name like GreenThumbAdventures.com would be fitting. After selecting your domain, choose a theme that reflects your style. Themes determine the layout and design of your blog, and most platforms offer both free and paid options.

Writing your first blog post is an exciting step. Begin by introducing yourself and explaining what readers can expect from your blog. Share your passions, interests, and what motivates you to write. Keep your tone conversational and engaging. Once your introduction is set, dive into your chosen topic. Whether it's a detailed account of your latest travel adventure or a step-by-step guide to planting roses, make sure your content is informative and enjoyable to read. Add photos or videos to make your posts visually appealing. When you're ready, hit the "Publish" button and share your post with the world.

Maintaining and growing a blog requires consistency and engagement. Create a content calendar to plan your posts. Decide how often you'll publish—weekly, bi-weekly, or monthly—and stick to your schedule. Regular posting keeps your readers engaged and coming back for more. Engage with your readers by responding to comments and questions. This interaction builds a sense of community and makes your readers feel valued. Share your posts on social media to reach a broader audience. Use SEO (Search Engine Optimization) techniques to make your blog more discoverable. This involves using relevant keywords, writing clear headings, and including links to reputable sources.

. . .

Consider the story of Carol, a retiree who started a travel blog. She began by documenting her trips to national parks, sharing stunning photos and detailed itineraries. Her blog gained a following as readers appreciated her insights and practical tips. Carol connected with other travel enthusiasts, exchanged advice, and even collaborated on group trips. Blogging enriched her travel experiences and introduced her to a supportive community of like-minded individuals.

Another inspiring example is Mike, who took up gardening after retirement and decided to blog about it. He shared his journey from novice to expert, posting everything from soil preparation to pest control. His blog became a valuable resource for fellow gardeners. Readers looked forward to his seasonal updates and practical advice. Blogging about his gardening adventures gave Mike a sense of purpose and allowed him to connect with others who shared his love for plants.

Blogging offers retirees a platform to share knowledge, connect with others, and document their experiences. It's a creative outlet that can be both personally rewarding and socially engaging. Whether you're passionate about travel, gardening, cooking, or any other interest, blogging can bring joy and fulfillment to your retirement years.

Using Apps for Health and Fitness Tracking

Imagine waking up each morning, checking your phone, and seeing a summary of your physical activity, sleep patterns, and progress toward your fitness goals. Health and fitness apps make this a reality, offering retirees a convenient way to stay active and monitor their health. These apps can track everything from your steps to your sleep quality, helping you set and achieve health and fitness goals. Whether you're looking to increase your daily activity, eat more healthily, or manage stress, there's an app that can help you succeed.

Let's start with tracking physical activity and exercise routines. Apps like Fitbit and Apple Health are excellent tools for this. Fitbit, for example, tracks your steps, distance, and calories burned throughout the day. Wear the Fitbit device, which syncs with your smartphone app. You can set daily step goals and receive reminders to move if you've been inactive for too long. Apple Health offers similar features, such as using your iPhone or Apple Watch to monitor your activity levels. Both apps provide detailed summaries of your physical activity, making it easy to see your progress and stay motivated.

Monitoring sleep patterns and quality is another significant benefit of these apps. Poor sleep can impact your overall health and well-being, so it's important to ensure you're getting enough restful sleep. Apps like Sleep Cycle and Fitbit track your sleep patterns, including the duration and quality of your sleep. Sleep Cycle uses your phone's microphone to analyze your sleep sounds and wake you up during your lightest sleep phase, making waking up easier and more pleasant. Fitbit devices monitor your sleep stages, providing insights into your time in light, deep, and REM sleep. These insights can help you adjust your sleep habits to improve sleep quality.

Setting and achieving health and fitness goals becomes much more manageable with the help of these apps. MyFitnessPal is a popular app for tracking nutrition and calories. By logging your meals and snacks, you can monitor your daily calorie intake and ensure you meet your nutritional needs. The app's extensive food database makes finding and logging your food easy; you can even scan barcodes for quick entry. Another benefit is that you can track your macronutrients, allowing you to understand the macro breakdown of the foods you consume. These macronutrients include carbohydrates, protein, and fat. MyFitnessPal also integrates with other fitness apps, allowing you to track your exercise and nutrition in one place.

For those interested in meditation and relaxation, apps like Calm and Headspace offer guided meditation sessions to help reduce stress and improve mental well-being. Calm provides various meditation programs, including sessions for beginners and more advanced practitioners. The app also features sleep stories, breathing exercises, and relaxing music. Headspace offers similar features, with guided meditation sessions focused on mindfulness, stress relief, and sleep improvement. These apps can be a valuable addition to your daily routine, helping you manage stress and maintain a positive mindset.

. . .

Integrating these apps into your daily routine is essential for consistency and long-term success. Start by setting daily step goals with your Fitbit or Apple Health app. Aim for at least 10,000 steps daily and track your progress. Use MyFitnessPal to log your meals and snacks, keeping an eye on your calorie intake and nutritional balance. Set reminders to log your food after each meal to ensure accuracy. Schedule regular meditation sessions with Calm or Headspace. Even five to ten minutes of meditation daily can significantly affect your stress levels and overall well-being.

Consider the story of Ned, a retiree who improved his fitness with a step tracker. Ned started using Fitbit to monitor his daily activity and set a goal of 10,000 steps per day. At first, he found it challenging to reach his goal, but the app's reminders and progress tracking kept him motivated. Over time, Ned increased his activity levels, incorporating daily walks and other forms of exercise into his routine. The result was improved physical fitness and a greater sense of accomplishment.

. . .

Another inspiring example is Jane, a retiree who used a meditation app for better sleep. Jane struggled with insomnia and often felt tired and irritable during the day. She decided to try the Calm app, starting with guided sleep meditations. The soothing voice and calming background sounds helped her relax and fall asleep more easily. After a few weeks of consistent use, Jane noticed a significant improvement in her sleep quality and overall mood. She felt more rested and energized, ready to enjoy her retirement to the fullest.

Integrating health and fitness apps into your daily routine can significantly enhance your well-being and help you achieve your fitness goals as a retiree. Whether it's tracking your physical activity, monitoring sleep quality, managing nutrition, or reducing stress through meditation, these tools offer convenient and effective ways to maintain your health. Apps like Fitbit, Apple Health, MyFitnessPal, Calm, and Headspace provide valuable insights and reminders that keep you motivated and on track. By embracing these technologies, retirees like Ned and Jane have successfully improved their physical fitness and mental well-being, showing that it's never too late to adopt a healthier lifestyle. It's all about creating routines and following them. This will allow you to experience improvements in your health and fitness goals.

Online Safety and Privacy Tips

Staying safe online is critical, especially as our daily activities move to the digital world. For retirees, understanding the importance of online safety and privacy can protect personal information and prevent scams. Recognizing phishing emails is a vital first step. These emails often look legitimate, mimicking trusted institutions like banks or government agencies. They might urge you to click a link or provide personal details. Look for signs like poor grammar, generic greetings, or suspicious email addresses. Contact the institution directly using a known phone number or website when in doubt.

Creating strong, unique passwords for online accounts is another critical aspect of online safety. Avoid using easily guessed passwords like "123456" or "password." Instead, opt for a combination of letters, numbers, and special characters. A password manager can help you keep track of complex passwords without remembering each one. Protecting personal information on social media is equally important. Be cautious about what you share. Scammers can use details like your full birthdate, address, or phone number to steal your identity. Adjust your privacy settings to limit who can see your posts and personal information.

Using two-factor authentication (2FA) adds an extra layer of security to your online accounts. This involves receiving a code by text or email that you must enter along with your password. It ensures that even someone with your password can't access your account without the secondary code. Installing antivirus software and keeping it updated is another practical step. This software can detect and remove malware, protecting your computer from threats. Avoid using public Wi-Fi for sensitive transactions like online banking. Public networks are less secure, making it easier for cybercriminals to intercept your data.

Online scams often target retirees, but awareness can help you avoid them. Phishing scams are emails or messages that trick you into providing personal information. Recognize these by checking for suspicious links or urgent requests for information. Fake online stores and offers are another scam. They might lure you with deals that seem too good to be true. Always research the store and read reviews before making a purchase. If you receive a suspicious email or come across a fraudulent website, report it. Most email providers have options to mark emails as spam or phishing. Reporting these issues helps protect others from falling victim.

One day, Margie received an email claiming to be from her bank, asking her to verify her account information. The email looked legitimate, but she noticed minor spelling errors and called her bank directly. They confirmed the email was a scam. Margie's vigilance and use of two-factor authentication protected her from potential fraud.

Another example is George, who stumbled upon a website offering high-end electronics at ridiculously low prices. Sensing something was off, he checked reviews and found numerous complaints about the site being a scam. He reported the site to his internet service provider and avoided a potential loss.

. . .

Staying safe online requires a combination of awareness and practical steps. Recognizing phishing emails and fraudulent websites can prevent you from falling victim to scams. Creating strong, unique passwords for your online accounts and using two-factor authentication adds an extra layer of protection. Be cautious about sharing personal information on social media, as oversharing can make you a target for identity theft. Installing and regularly updating antivirus software keeps your devices secure from malware and other threats. Avoid using public Wi-Fi for sensitive transactions to ensure your data remains private. Reporting suspicious emails or websites helps protect yourself and others who might be less vigilant. The digital world offers many conveniences, but it also comes with risks. Taking these precautions can help you enjoy the benefits of technology without compromising your safety.

Virtual Socializing: Zoom and Beyond

You are sitting in your cozy living room, connecting face-to-face with your grandkids who live states away, or catching up with old friends over a virtual coffee. Doesn't this sound good? For retirees, video conferencing tools like Zoom, Skype, and Google Meet have become invaluable for connecting with loved ones and engaging in social activities. These platforms allow you to participate in family gatherings, join virtual events, and even take online classes, all from the comfort of your home.

To get started with Zoom, visit the Zoom website and click "Sign Up, It's Free." Enter your email address and follow the prompts to create your account. Once you've set up your profile, you can schedule a meeting by clicking "Schedule a Meeting" and filling in the details like date, time, and meeting topic. Invite participants by sending them the meeting link via email. When it's time for the meeting, click "Start," and you're ready to go. Zoom's user-friendly interface can mute/unmute your microphone, turn your camera on/off, and share your screen if needed.

Skype is another excellent option for video calls and messaging. Download the Skype app from your device's app store and sign up using your email or phone number. Once your account is set up, you can add contacts by searching for their

Skype usernames or email addresses. To make a video call, click on the contact's name and the video call button. Skype also offers instant messaging, allowing you to send text messages, photos, and files during your call.

Google Meet is an excellent choice for those who prefer group video chats. If you have a Gmail account, you already have access to Google Meet. Open your Gmail and click the "Meet" icon on the left sidebar. Click "New Meeting" to start a session and invite participants by sharing the meeting link. Google Meet supports larger groups and offers features like screen sharing and real-time captions, making it ideal for virtual social gatherings and classes.

When it comes to virtual socializing, setting up a comfortable and well-lit space is important. Choose a quiet area in your home where you won't be disturbed. Good lighting is essential; natural light is best, but a well-placed lamp can also do the trick. Position your camera at eye level to ensure a flattering angle. Using headphones can improve audio quality and reduce background noise. Engage actively in virtual discussions by making eye contact with the camera, nodding, and responding to others' comments. Show interest by asking questions and sharing your thoughts.

Consider the story of Jack, who hosts regular Zoom calls with his family. Every Sunday, his children and grandchildren join a virtual family gathering with games and storytelling. This ritual has become a cherished part of their week, keeping everyone connected despite the distance. Then there's Mary, who joined a virtual book club on Google Meet. She loves discussing her favorite novels with fellow book enthusiasts, sharing insights, and discovering new reads. These virtual interactions have enriched her social life and provided a sense of community.

Virtual socializing offers a lifeline for retirees, ensuring that physical distance doesn't translate into social isolation. By embracing video conferencing tools, you can maintain and even expand your social network, participate in enriching activities, and stay connected with loved ones. Whether you're catching up with family, attending a virtual class, or joining an online group, these platforms make it all possible.

. . .

This chapter explored how mastering digital skills can enhance your retirement experience, from staying socially connected to pursuing new hobbies and protecting your online presence. These skills open up a world of possibilities, making your retirement years fulfilling and exciting. Next, we'll dive into ways to keep your brain healthy and your outlook optimistic.

10
MENTAL WELL-BEING AND MINDFULNESS

"Although the world is full of suffering, it is full also of the overcoming of it."

— HELEN KELLER

Envision waking up each morning with calm and clarity, ready to embrace the day with a peaceful mind. This is the power of meditation—a practice that has been used for centuries to help individuals find inner peace and balance. For many, retirement brings a mix of excitement and uncertainty. The newfound freedom can sometimes lead to feelings of anxiety and restlessness. Meditation offers a way to navigate these emotions, providing a sanctuary of calm amid the changes. It's a tool that can reduce stress, improve focus, and enhance overall mental well-being, making it an invaluable addition to your daily routine. This chapter will explore meditation and other ways to keep your brain and mind strong and balanced.

Meditation Techniques for Beginners

Meditation is more than just sitting quietly; it's a practice that involves focusing your mind, relaxing your body, and redirecting your thoughts. One of the most significant benefits of meditation is its ability to reduce anxiety and promote relaxation. By focusing on your breath and the present moment, you can calm your mind and let go of worries. This practice helps in lowering stress levels, which in turn can have a profound impact on your overall health. The National Institutes of Health reports that the number of adults practicing meditation has increased significantly, highlighting its growing popularity and effectiveness.

In addition to reducing anxiety, meditation can also improve concentration and mental clarity. Training your mind to focus on one thing at a time can enhance your ability to concentrate on tasks and make decisions more effectively. This improved focus can be especially beneficial in retirement when distractions and a lack of structure can sometimes make it challenging to stay on track. Meditation also enhances emotional health by helping you connect with your inner self. It allows you to explore and understand your emotions, promoting emotional resilience and stability.

You don't need any special equipment or prior experience to get started with meditation. One simple and accessible method is mindfulness meditation, which involves focusing on the present moment without judgment. Find a quiet space where you won't be disturbed. Sit comfortably, close your eyes, and take a few deep breaths. Begin by paying attention to your breath as it goes in and out. If your mind wanders, gently bring your focus back to your breath. This practice helps you stay grounded and aware of the present moment.

Another effective technique is guided meditation, which is a simple, accessible way to experience relaxation and improve mental well-being. It involves listening to a guide, often through an audio recording, who leads you through calming imagery, breathing exercises, or mindfulness practices. This can help reduce stress, improve focus, and promote emotional balance. Guided meditation offers a gentle way to enhance mental clarity, lower anxiety, and even improve sleep, making it an excellent tool for maintaining both mental and physical health in retirement.

Loving-kindness meditation is another beautiful practice that involves cultivating compassion and kindness toward yourself and others. Begin by sitting comfortably and taking a few deep breaths. Imagine sending positive thoughts and wishes to yourself, such as "May I be happy, healthy, and at peace." Next, extend these wishes to your loved ones, friends, and even people you may have conflicts with. This practice helps to foster a sense of connection and empathy, enhancing emotional well-being and reducing negative emotions.

Like any new practice, meditation can come with its challenges. One common issue is dealing with restlessness and distractions. It's normal for your mind to wander, especially when you're just starting. Instead of getting frustrated, gently guide your focus back to your breath or the guided meditation. Remember, the goal is not to empty your mind but to become aware of your thoughts and gently redirect them. Setting a regular meditation schedule can also help. Choose a specific time each day to meditate, whether in the morning, afternoon, or evening. Consistency is key to developing a lasting practice.

Finding a comfortable meditation space is also important. Choose a quiet spot in your home where you can sit undisturbed for a few minutes. This space doesn't have to be elaborate; a simple corner with a cushion or chair will do. The important thing is that it's a place where you feel relaxed and at ease. Over time, this space can become a sanctuary where you can retreat to find peace and clarity.

Consider the story of Judy, a retiree who struggled with anxiety after leaving the workforce. She decided to try mindfulness meditation to help manage her stress. Judy would sit in her favorite chair by the window every morning, close her eyes, and focus on her breathing. At first, she found it challenging to quiet her mind, but she noticed a difference with consistent practice. Judy felt more relaxed and less anxious throughout the day. Her newfound calm allowed her to enjoy her retirement more fully and engage in activities she once found overwhelming.

Another inspiring example is Mark, who used guided meditation to improve his focus. Mark had always been a busy professional, and the sudden shift to a slower pace in retirement left him feeling restless and unfocused. He discovered a guided meditation app and started incorporating short sessions into his daily routine. The guided voice helped him stay focused and provided structure to his practice. Over time, Mark noticed that his concentration improved and that he felt more present and engaged in daily activities.

Meditation Practice Checklist

1. **Find a quiet space.** Choose a spot where you can sit undisturbed.
2. **Sit comfortably.** Use a cushion or chair to support your posture.

3. **Set a timer.** Start with 5–10 minutes and gradually increase the duration.
4. **Focus on your breath.** Pay attention to the sensation of breathing.
5. **Use guided meditation.** Explore apps like Calm and Headspace for assistance.
6. **Practice loving-kindness.** Send positive thoughts to yourself and others.
7. **Be consistent.** Meditate at the same time each day.
8. **Stay patient.** Gently bring your focus back if your mind wanders.

∼

Meditation is a powerful tool that can bring immense benefits to your retirement. It helps reduce stress, improve focus, and enhance emotional health, making navigating the ups and downs of this new chapter in life more manageable. Whether you choose mindfulness meditation, guided meditation, or loving-kindness meditation, the key is to start and stay consistent. Over time, you'll find that meditation becomes a cherished part of your daily routine, offering a sanctuary of calm and clarity.

Engaging in Brain Games and Puzzles

Picture sitting in your favorite chair, a crossword puzzle spread out in front of you, pencil in hand. You feel a sense of satisfaction as you fill in each word, the clues sparking memories and challenging your mind. Brain games and puzzles offer a delightful way to keep your cognitive health in check. They do more than just pass the time; they enhance mental sharpness and delay cognitive decline. These activities can significantly improve memory and problem-solving skills, making everyday tasks more enjoyable. Additionally, they encourage critical thinking and creativity, providing an ongoing mental workout that keeps your brain agile and engaged.

Crossword puzzles, for example, are a fantastic way to enhance vocabulary and improve memory. Each clue requires you to recall information, make connections, and think critically. Similarly, word searches can help improve focus and attention to detail as you scan the grid for hidden words. These puzzles provide mental stimulation and a sense of accomplishment when you find that elusive word or complete the grid.

. . .

Sudoku and other number puzzles are excellent for boosting logical thinking and problem-solving abilities. Sudoku involves filling a grid with numbers so that each row, column, and smaller grid contains all the digits from 1 to 9. This requires concentration, strategic thinking, and patience. The elimination and logical deduction process used in Sudoku can help sharpen your mind and improve cognitive functions. Other number puzzles, such as Kakuro or KenKen, offer similar benefits, challenging your mathematical skills and enhancing your ability to think logically.

Logic and strategy games like chess and checkers are also incredibly beneficial for cognitive health. Chess, known as the "game of kings," requires strategic planning, foresight, and anticipating your opponent's moves. Each game is a mental battle that hones your critical thinking and decision-making skills. Checkers, while simpler, still requires strategic thinking and planning. These games provide a fun and engaging way to keep your mind sharp and agile.

Incorporating brain games into your daily routine is valuable for maintaining cognitive health. Just as physical exercise keeps your body fit, mental exercise keeps your brain in top shape. Set aside time each day for a brain game or puzzle. This could be a morning crossword with your coffee, a Sudoku puzzle during your afternoon break, or an evening chess game. The key is consistency. Regular mental exercise can help keep your mind sharp and delay cognitive decline.

Joining puzzle clubs or online communities can also enhance your experience. These groups provide a platform to share puzzles, compete in challenges, and connect with like-minded individuals. Engaging with others adds a social element to your mental workout, making it more enjoyable and motivating. Puzzle clubs often organize events and competitions, providing an opportunity to test your skills and learn new strategies.

Challenging yourself with progressively more complex puzzles is another effective way to keep your mind sharp. Start with easier puzzles and gradually move on to more difficult ones. This progression keeps your brain challenged and engaged, preventing it from becoming complacent. Each new level of difficulty requires you to think more critically and creatively, further enhancing your cognitive abilities.

Consider the story of Alice, a retiree who found joy and mental stimulation in daily crossword puzzles. Alice started with simple puzzles and gradually moved on to more challenging ones. She noticed improvements in her memory and problem-solving skills, making her feel more confident and mentally agile. Working on crossword puzzles became a cherished part of her routine, providing mental stimulation and a sense of accomplishment.

Another inspiring example is Arthur, who joined a local chess club after retirement. Arthur had always been interested in chess but never had the time to pursue it seriously. The chess club provided a supportive community where he could learn new strategies and compete with others. Arthur's strategic thinking and decision-making skills improved significantly, and he formed lasting friendships with fellow club members. The mental challenge of each game kept his mind sharp and engaged, adding a new dimension of fulfillment to his retirement.

. . .

Brain games and puzzles offer a fun and effective way to maintain cognitive health in retirement. They improve memory, enhance problem-solving skills, and encourage critical thinking and creativity. By incorporating these activities into your daily routine, joining puzzle clubs or online communities, and challenging yourself with progressively more complex puzzles, you can keep your mind sharp and engaged, making your retirement years both enjoyable and mentally stimulating.

∼

Brain Games Resource List

1. **Crossword Puzzles:** Available in newspapers, puzzle books, and online platforms like The New York Times Crossword.
2. **Word Searches:** Find themed word search books or online versions on websites like Puzzle Baron.
3. **Sudoku:** Accessible in newspapers, puzzle books, and apps like Sudoku.com.

4. **Logic and Strategy Games:** Play chess on platforms like Chess.com or checkers on 247Checkers.com.
5. **Brain Training Apps:** Try Lumosity or Elevate for a variety of cognitive exercises.
6. **Puzzle Clubs:** Join local clubs or online communities like the American Crossword Puzzle Tournament.

∼

Engaging in brain games and puzzles can significantly improve your cognitive health, making your retirement years fulfilling and mentally stimulating. So, grab that crossword puzzle or download a brain training app, and start exercising your mind today.

Practicing Gratitude and Positive Thinking

Imagine starting each day with a heart full of gratitude and a mind tuned to positive thoughts. This shift in perspective can profoundly impact your mental well-being, making your retirement years more joyful and satisfying. Gratitude and positive thinking are not just trendy buzzwords; they are powerful tools that can enhance happiness, reduce stress, and promote emotional resilience.

Cultivating a positive mindset can significantly improve your overall life satisfaction. When you focus on the good things in your life, you begin to see more of them. This doesn't mean ignoring challenges or pretending everything is perfect. Instead, it's about finding the silver linings and appreciating the small joys that often go unnoticed. By doing so, you can reduce symptoms of depression and anxiety, paving the way for a more content and peaceful state of mind.

One practical way to practice gratitude is by keeping a gratitude journal. Each day, take a few minutes to write down things you are thankful for. These can be as simple as a sunny day, a kind word from a friend, or a delicious meal. The act of writing helps reinforce these positive experiences in your mind, creating a habit of noticing and appreciating the good in your life. Over time, this practice can shift your focus from what's lacking to what's abundant, enhancing your overall sense of well-being.

. . .

Expressing gratitude to others is an effective method. This can be done through thank-you notes, verbal acknowledgments, or even small acts of kindness. Letting people know you appreciate them strengthens your relationships and boosts your mood. When you express gratitude, you create a positive feedback loop that enhances your happiness and that of those around you.

Reflecting on positive experiences is also useful. Take time to savor and appreciate joyful moments. Whether it's a walk in the park, a phone call with a loved one, or a favorite hobby, thoroughly enjoying these moments can enhance your happiness. Reflecting on these experiences helps solidify them in your memory, making recalling and reliving them easier during challenging times.

Developing a positive mindset involves shifting your focus from negative to positive aspects of life. One effective strategy is reframing negative thoughts. When faced with a challenging situation, try to find something positive about it. This could be a lesson learned, a new opportunity, or simply the fact that you have the strength to face it. Reframing helps you see situations differently, reducing their emotional impact.

Practicing self-compassion is another vital component. Be kind and understanding toward yourself, especially during difficult times. Instead of criticizing yourself for mistakes or shortcomings, treat yourself with the same kindness and understanding you would offer a friend. Self-compassion fosters emotional resilience and helps you bounce back from setbacks more quickly.

Surrounding yourself with positivity is essential. Engage in activities and relationships that uplift and inspire you. This could be spending time with supportive friends, pursuing hobbies that bring you joy, or participating in community events. Positive environments and relationships can significantly enhance your mood and overall outlook on life.

Helen is a retiree who struggled with loneliness and sadness after leaving her job. She started a daily gratitude journal, writing down three things she was thankful for each day. Initially, finding things to be grateful for was challenging, but as she continued the practice, it became easier. Helen began to notice the small joys in her life, like her garden's beauty or a neighbor's friendly smile. Over time, her mood improved, and she felt more content and at peace.

Another inspiring example is Tom, who cultivated a positive mindset through self-compassion practices. Tom had always been hard on himself, often focusing on his perceived failures and shortcomings. After learning about self-compassion, he began treating himself with kindness and understanding. When he made a mistake, instead of criticizing himself, he acknowledged it as part of being human and focused on what he could learn from the experience. This shift in mindset helped Tom become more resilient and happier, improving his overall mental well-being.

Gratitude and positive thinking are powerful tools that can enhance your mental well-being, making your retirement years more fulfilling and joyful. By practicing gratitude, expressing it to others, reflecting on positive experiences, and developing a positive mindset, you can create a life filled with happiness and contentment. These practices promote emotional resilience, enhance life satisfaction, and reduce symptoms of depression and anxiety, helping you navigate the challenges of retirement with grace and positivity.

This chapter explored the significant impact of mental well-being and mindfulness on your life. Each practice offers unique benefits, from meditation techniques to brain games and the power of gratitude. These tools can enhance your mental health, making your retirement years more fulfilling and joyful.

Take the First Step Toward Building a Dynamic Community of Like-Minded Seniors

You may miss your work friends and make it a point to catch up with them, but I hope these pages have shown you that there is a bustling, busy community of seniors waiting to meet you. There are so many places where you can meet fascinating, intelligent, fun-loving seniors you never had a chance to come across.

Think community workshops, language learning classes, and volunteering activities. This book has cast a wide net and presented you with a myriad of ideas to explore, and I hope you get started today! Before you end your journey through these pages, however, please leave a sentence or two to help other seniors wishing to make their retirement the most fulfilling time of their lives.

Thank you for your help. I wish you many new connections, experiences, and travels...there is so much of the world to explore, but I hope the most fascinating discovery you make is yourself!

Click here to leave your review on Amazon.

Scan the QR code below

CONCLUSION

As you stand at the threshold of this new chapter in your life, it's essential to take a moment to reflect on the journey we've taken together. The transition into retirement can be both exhilarating and daunting, but with the right mindset and a wealth of activities to choose from, it can become the most fulfilling period of your life!

We delved into rediscovering yourself by uncovering hidden passions and setting personal goals. You learned how to create a vision board and use journaling as a tool for self-discovery. Embracing a growth mindset and setting achievable milestones can guide you toward continuous personal growth and satisfaction.

Social connections are vital for a vibrant retirement. We explored ways to join local clubs, host themed gatherings, and use technology to stay connected. You discovered the joy of starting or joining a book club and the fulfillment of volunteering for social good. These activities not only keep you engaged but also enrich your social life.

Travel and adventure offer endless possibilities for exploration. Whether it's planning budget-friendly road trips, embarking on international volunteer vacations, or joining group tours and cruises, the world is at your fingertips. Adventure travel and cultural immersion trips provide unique experiences that add excitement and depth to your retirement.

Creative and artistic pursuits can bring immense joy and a sense of accomplishment. From painting and drawing to writing your memoirs, crafting with recycled materials, and capturing life's moments through photography, these activities allow you to express yourself and discover hidden talents. Learning an instrument or exploring dance styles can add a rhythmic and musical dimension to your days.

Maintaining your health and fitness is crucial for enjoying all these activities. We discussed low-impact exercises for joint health, the benefits of yoga and meditation, and the rejuvenating effects of swimming and water aerobics. Joining walking or hiking groups and following nutrition tips for active seniors can keep you fit and energetic.

Lifelong learning keeps your mind sharp and engaged. Enrolling in online courses, attending local workshops, learning new languages, and exploring history through local museums are excellent ways to continue growing intellectually. Community college classes offer diverse opportunities to expand your knowledge and skills.

Financial peace of mind ensures that you can enjoy your retirement without worry. We covered budgeting for your new lifestyle, exploring part-time work and freelance opportunities, maximizing Social Security benefits, and smart investing. Downsizing and simplifying your home can reduce expenses and enhance your living environment.

Mastering technology and digital skills can open up new avenues for connection and learning. Social media platforms, blogging, health and fitness apps, and virtual socializing tools can enrich your daily life. Online safety and privacy tips ensure that you enjoy these benefits securely.

Lastly, mental well-being and mindfulness are the cornerstones of a fulfilling retirement. Meditation techniques, brain games, and practicing gratitude and positive thinking can enhance mental health, reduce stress, and promote a positive outlook.

As you embark on this journey, remember that retirement is not the end but a new beginning. It's a time to rediscover yourself, build meaningful connections, explore the world, and engage in activities that bring you joy and fulfillment. The possibilities are endless, and the choice is yours.

Take action today. Pick up that paintbrush, join that book club, plan that road trip, or simply take a moment to meditate. Each step brings you closer to a retirement filled with purpose and happiness.

You deserve a retirement that includes living longer AND better. Embrace this opportunity with open arms and a curious heart. Surround yourself with positivity, stay active, and keep learning. Your best years are ahead of you; every day is a chance to create new memories and experiences.

As you move forward, remember Helen Keller's words: "Life is either a daring adventure or nothing at all." Make your retirement the adventure of a lifetime. You have the tools, the inspiration, and the determination to make it so. Enjoy every moment, and may this new chapter be the most rewarding yet!

REFERENCES

"5 Self-Discovery Activities | Relationships Australia QLD." https://www.raq.org.au/blog/5-self-discovery-activities-try-weekend.

"7 Best Apps for Cheap Accommodation in 2024," April 8, 2023. https://notanotherbackpacker.com/en/apps-for-cheap-accommodation/.

AARP. "15 Part-Time Jobs for Retirees (No Degree Required!)." https://www.aarp.org/work/job-search/retiree-part-time-jobs/.

Amy. "Easy Recycled Crafts." DIY Candy, June 7, 2024. https://diycandy.com/easy-recycled-crafts/.

Balkhi, Syed. "How to Start a WordPress Blog in 2024 (Beginner's Guide)," September 15, 2016. https://www.wpbeginner.com/start-a-wordpress-blog/.

"Beyond Bob Ross: 9 Tips for Seniors Who Want to Take Up a Painting Hobby." https://www.bethesdagardensfrisco.com/blog/beyond-bob-ross-9-tips-for-seniors-who-want-to-take-up-a-painting-hobby.

Connect Safely. "The Senior's Guide to Online Safety," August 25, 2021. https://connectsafely.org/seniors-guide-to-online-safety/.

Eldwell. "The Benefits of Joining Senior Clubs and Social Groups | Eldwell Guardian." https://eldwell.com/the-benefits-of-joining-senior-clubs-and-social-groups.

"Friendship | Successful Seniors: 10 Stories of Purpose Discovered Later in Life | News & Insights." https://www.friendship.us/insights/successful-seniors.

Hartman, Rachel. "Volunteer Opportunities for Seniors." U.S. News, December 7, 2023. https://money.usnews.com/

money/retirement/aging/articles/volunteer-opportunities-for-seniors.

HumanGood. "7 Low Impact Exercises for Older Adults to Stay Active." https://www.humangood.org/resources/senior-living-blog/low-impact-exercises-for-older-adults.

International Volunteer HQ. "A Senior's Volunteer Adventure & The Road To a Fulfilling Retirement," November 3, 2021. https://www.volunteerhq.org/blog/senior-volunteer-abroad-story/.

"Journaling for Seniors: How It Enhances Your Brain Health." https://www.seniorhelpers.com/ca/san-mateo/resources/blogs/journaling-for-seniors-how-it-enhances-your-brain-health/.

Lifestyle, Senior. "10 Healthy Benefits of Meditation for Seniors." Senior Lifestyle, September 17, 2013. https://www.seniorlifestyle.com/resources/blog/healthy-benefits-of-meditation-for-seniors/.

Lynch, Brian. "Retiree Finds a More Fulfilling Journey through the Peace Corps." Peace Corps, February 16, 2023. https://www.peacecorps.gov/stories/retiree-finds-a-more-fulfilling-journey-through-the-peace-corps/.

Madhivanan, Purnima, Karl Krupp, Randall Waechter, and Rahu Shidhaye. "Yoga for Healthy Aging: Science or Hype?" *Advances in Geriatric Medicine and Research* 3, no. 3 (2021): e210016. https://doi.org/10.20900/agmr20210016.

McGough, Nellah Bailey. 2024. "75 Retirement Quotes That Will Resonate With Any Retiree." Southern Living. April 25, 2024. https://www.southernliving.com/culture/retirement-quotes.

Northwestern Mutual. "5 Road Trips for Budget-Minded Retirees." https://www.northwesternmutual.com/life-and-money/5-budget-minded-road-trips-for-retirees/.

Road Scholar. "Outdoor Adventure Tours for Seniors." https://www.roadscholar.org/collections/outdoor-adventures/.

Roth, Emma. "The 10 Best Websites to Find Volunteer Work

and Opportunities." MUO, August 23, 2019. https://www.makeuseof.com/tag/websites-find-volunteer-work/.

sageage. "How Seniors Benefit from Lifelong Learning." The Delaney at The Green, February 20, 2024. https://delaneyatthegreen.com/blog/2024/02/20/the-benefits-of-lifelong-learning-in-retirement/.

Sandberg, Erica. "9 Money Apps to Keep Your Retirement Planning on Track." U.S. News, September 25, 2023. https://money.usnews.com/money/retirement/articles/money-apps-to-keep-your-retirement-planning-on-track.

SeniorResource. "Senior Education." https://www.seniorresource.com/senior-education/.

Sheffler, Pamela, Esra Kürüm, Angelica M. Sheen, Annie S. Ditta, Leah Ferguson, Diamond Bravo, George W. Rebok, Carla M. Strickland-Hughes, and Rachel Wu. "Growth Mindset Predicts Cognitive Gains in an Older Adult Multi-Skill Learning Intervention." *International Journal of Aging & Human Development* 96, no. 4 (June 2023): 501–26. https://doi.org/10.1177/00914150221106095.

SilverSneakers. "Discover the Best Free Exercise Apps for Seniors in 2024," April 15, 2024. https://www.silversneakers.com/blog/8-best-fitness-apps-for-older-adults/.

SilverSneakers. "Is Swimming the World's Best Exercise?," March 19, 2024. https://www.silversneakers.com/blog/swimming-exercise/.

Soriano, Deborah Ziff. "Create a Vision Board for a Picture-Perfect Retirement." Citi Life and Money, July 3, 2024. https://www.lifeandmoney.citi.com/lam/articles/milestones/retirement/vision-board-retirement

Stott, Juliet. "Downsizing for Retirement: Real Stories." *The Guardian*, July 28, 2015, sec. Money. https://www.theguardian.com/money/2015/jul/28/downsizing-for-retirement-real-stories.

Strettner, Morey. "How to Write a Memoir, According to Retirees Who Have Actually Done It." Market Watch, February 24, 2024. https://www.marketwatch.com/story/how-to-write-a-memoir-according-to-retirees-who-have-actually-done-it-e8031220.

Taherkhani, Zahra, Mohammad Hossein Kaveh, Arash Mani, Leila Ghahremani, and Khadijeh Khademi. "The Effect of Positive Thinking on Resilience and Life Satisfaction of Older Adults: A Randomized Controlled Trial." *Scientific Reports* 13 (March 1, 2023): 3478. https://doi.org/10.1038/s41598-023-30684-y.

"USDA MyPlate Nutrition Information for Older Adults." https://www.myplate.gov/life-stages/older-adults.

Verywell Mind. "Keep Your Brain Young and Sharp With These 10 Games." https://www.verywellmind.com/top-web sites-and-games-for-brain-exercise-2224140.

Volunteer Forever. "Volunteer Abroad Opportunities for Seniors and Retirees." https://www.volunteerforever.com/article_post/volunteer-abroad-opportunities-for-seniors-and-retirees/.

Walton, Stephen. "Top 10 Photography Tips for Beginners Over 50." *Online Photography Courses from iPhotography* (blog), August 6, 2024. https://www.iphotography.com/blog/top-10-photography-tips-for-beginners-over-50/.

Made in the USA
Columbia, SC
17 April 2025